The Infectious Disease Colouring Book

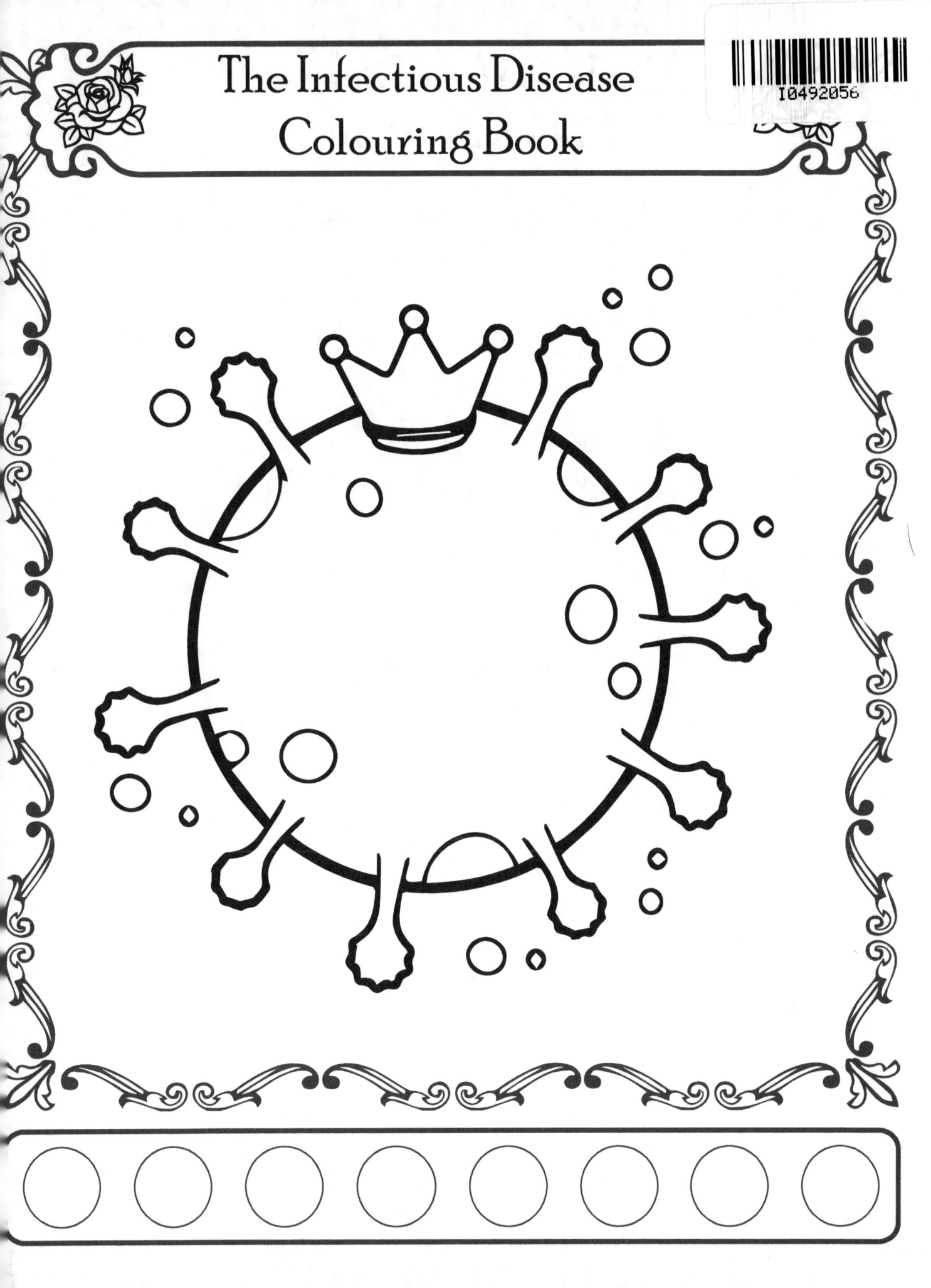

The Infectious Disease Colouring Book

The Infectious Disease Colouring Book

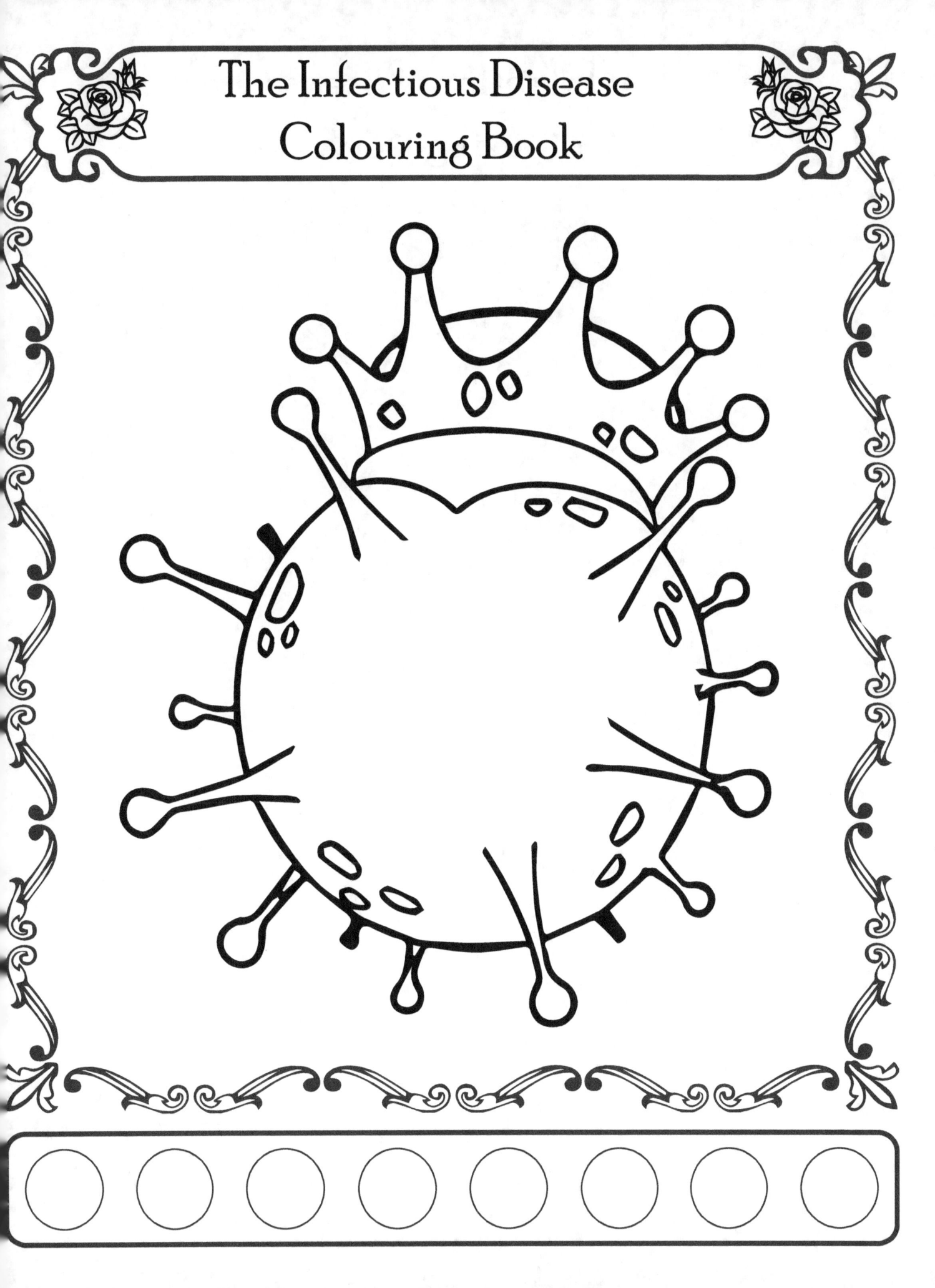

The Infectious Disease Colouring Book

The Infectious Disease Colouring Book

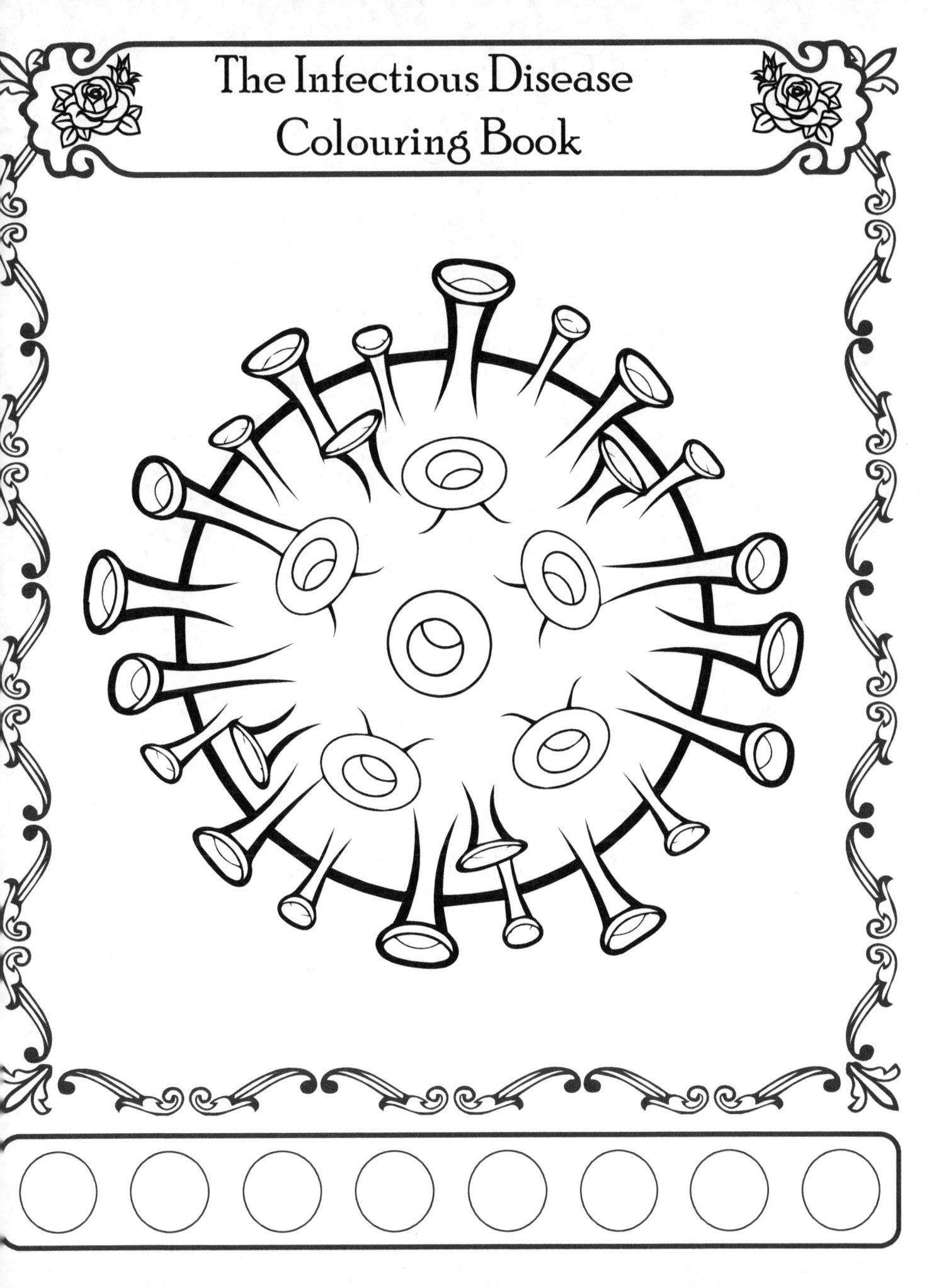

The Infectious Disease Colouring Book

The Infectious Disease Colouring Book

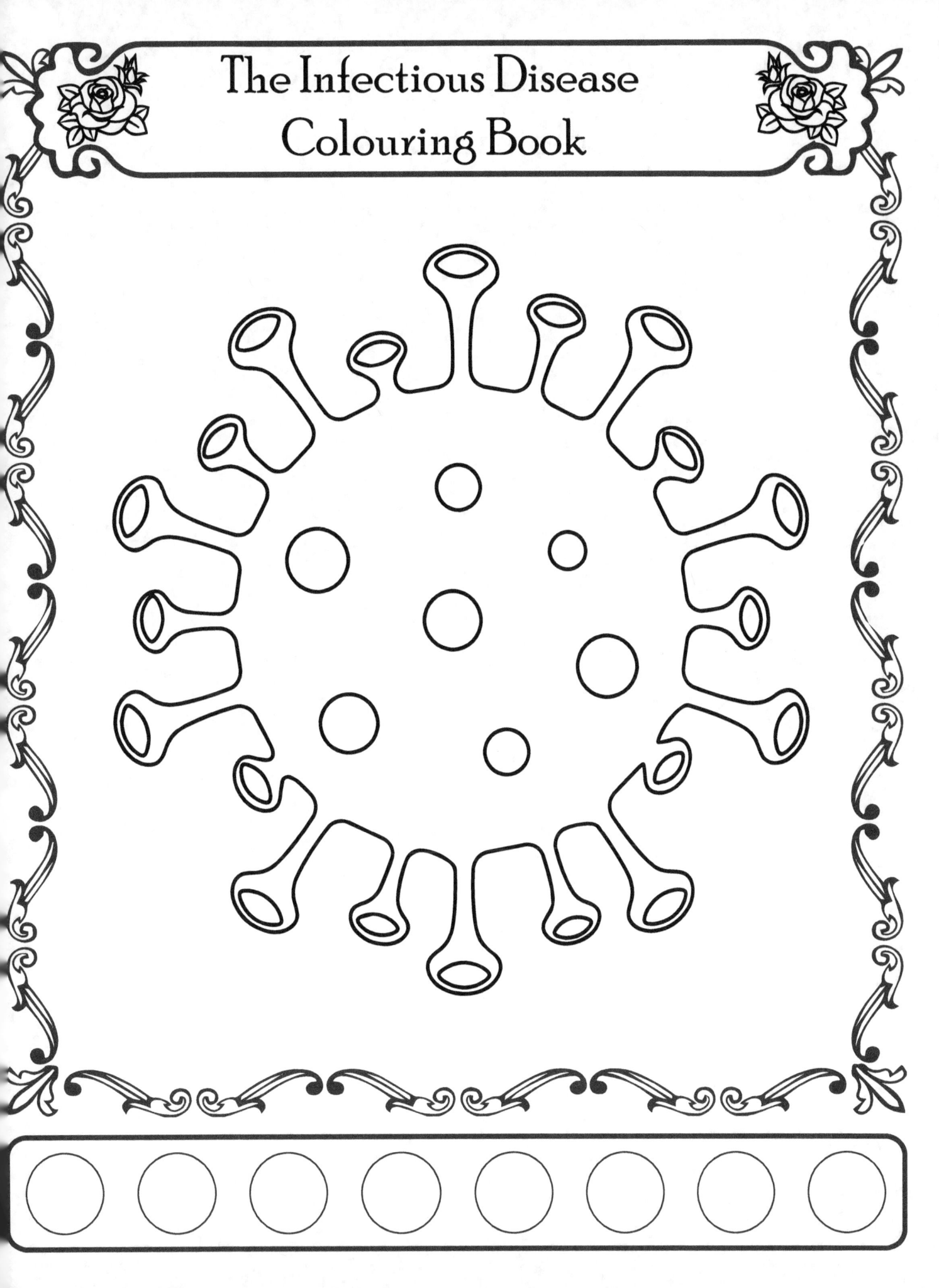

The Infectious Disease
Colouring Book

The Infectious Disease Colouring Book

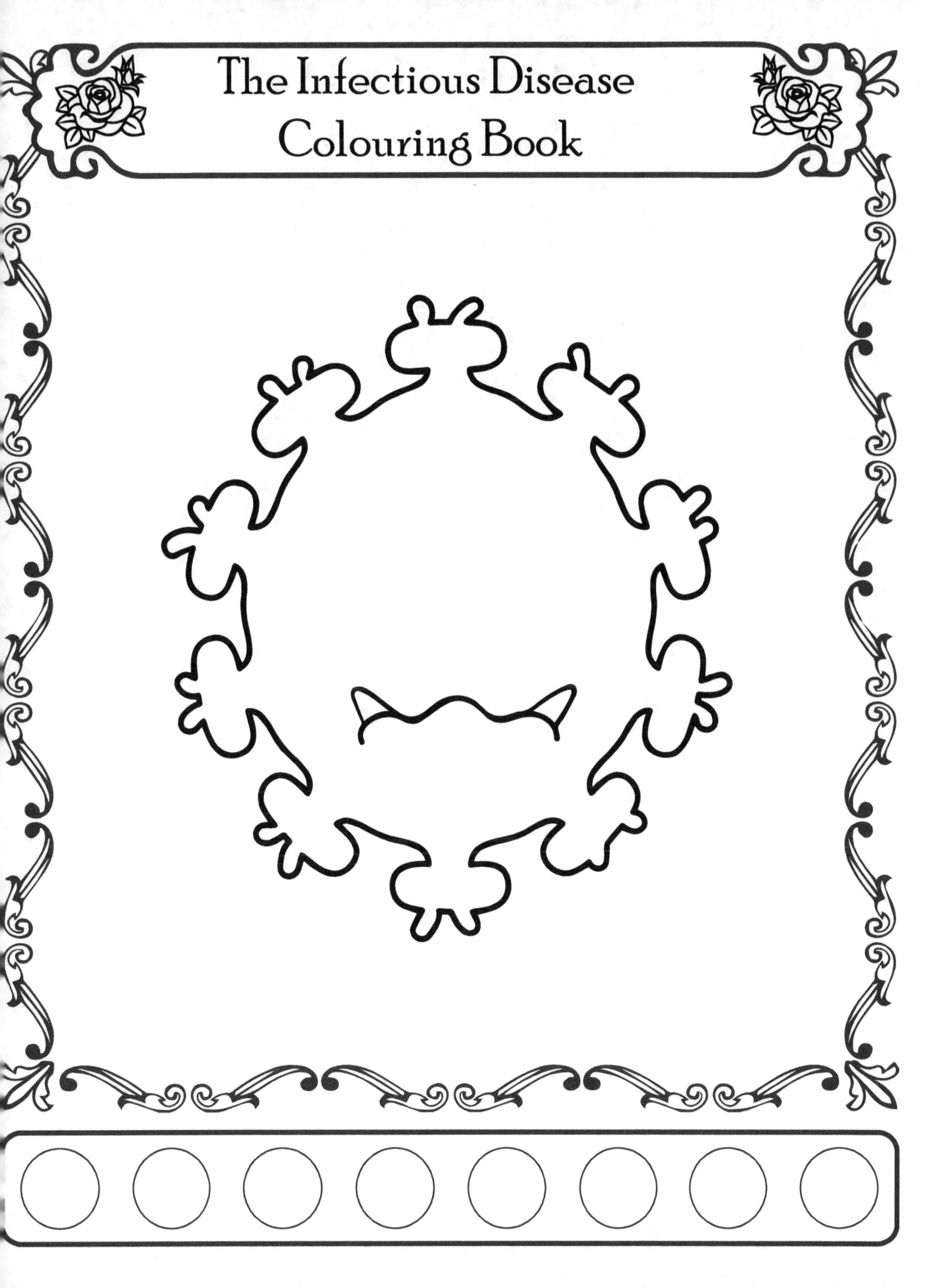

The Infectious Disease Colouring Book

The Infectious Disease Colouring Book

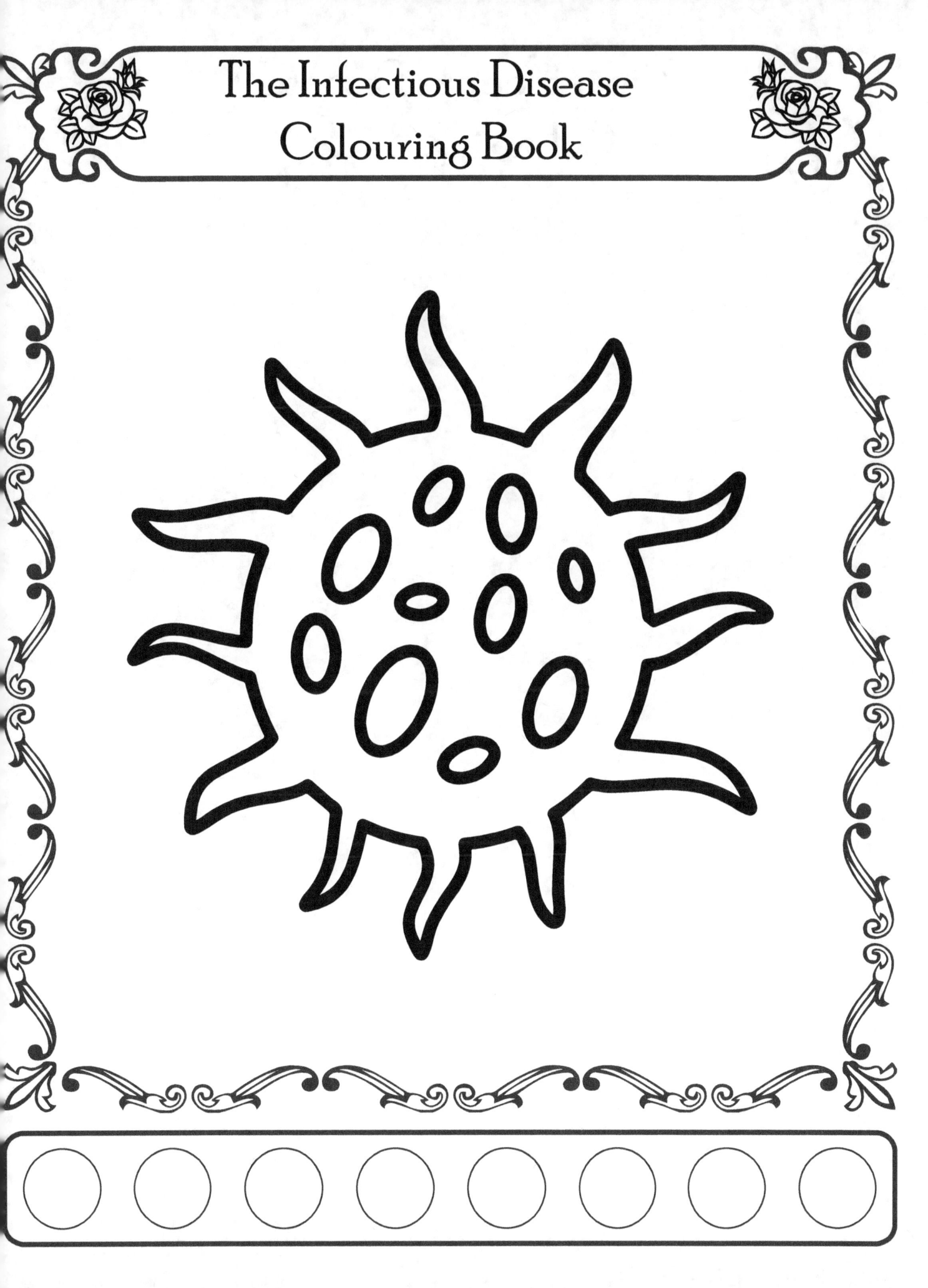

The Infectious Disease Colouring Book

The Infectious Disease Colouring Book

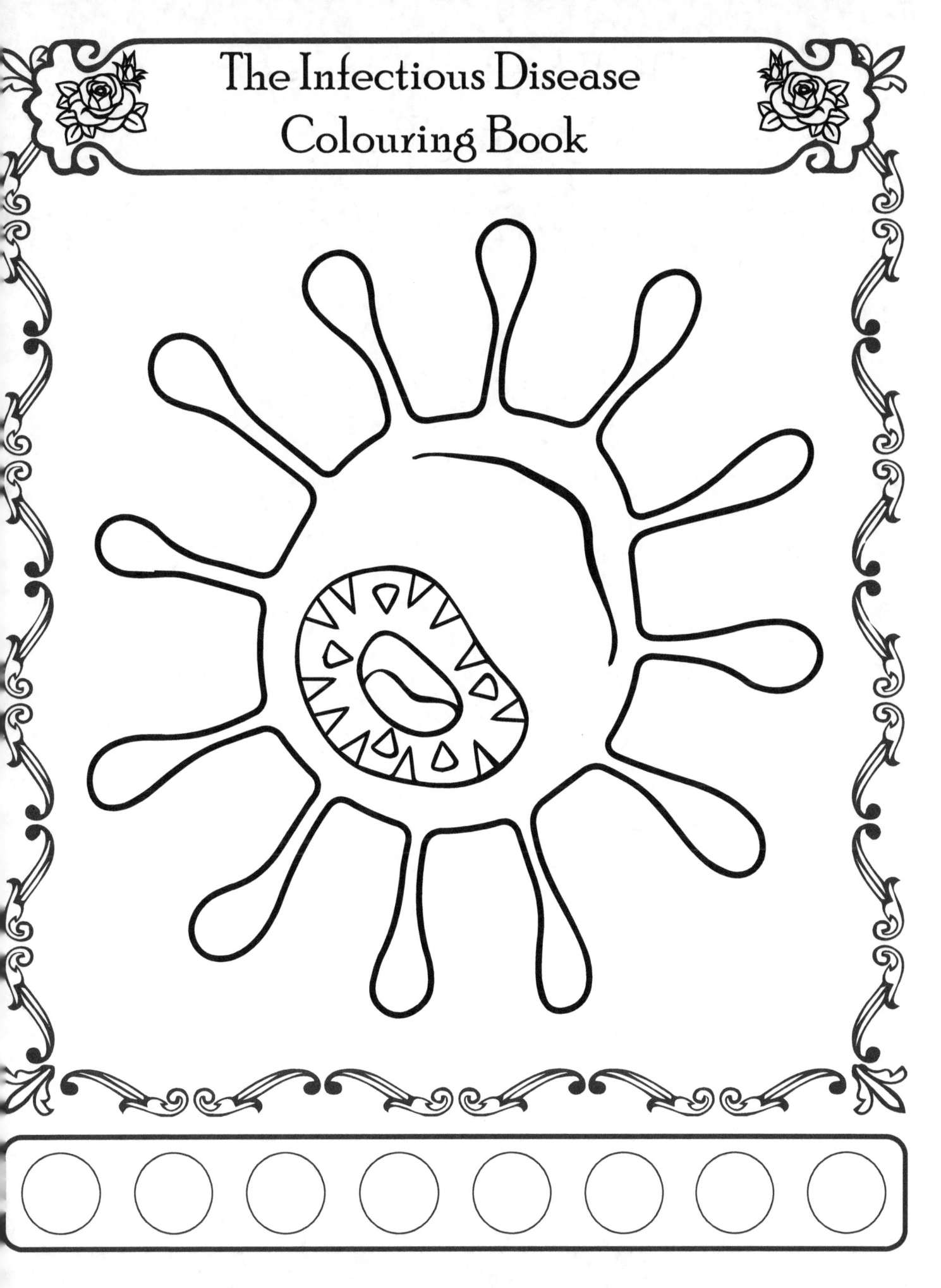

The Infectious Disease Colouring Book

The Infectious Disease Colouring Book

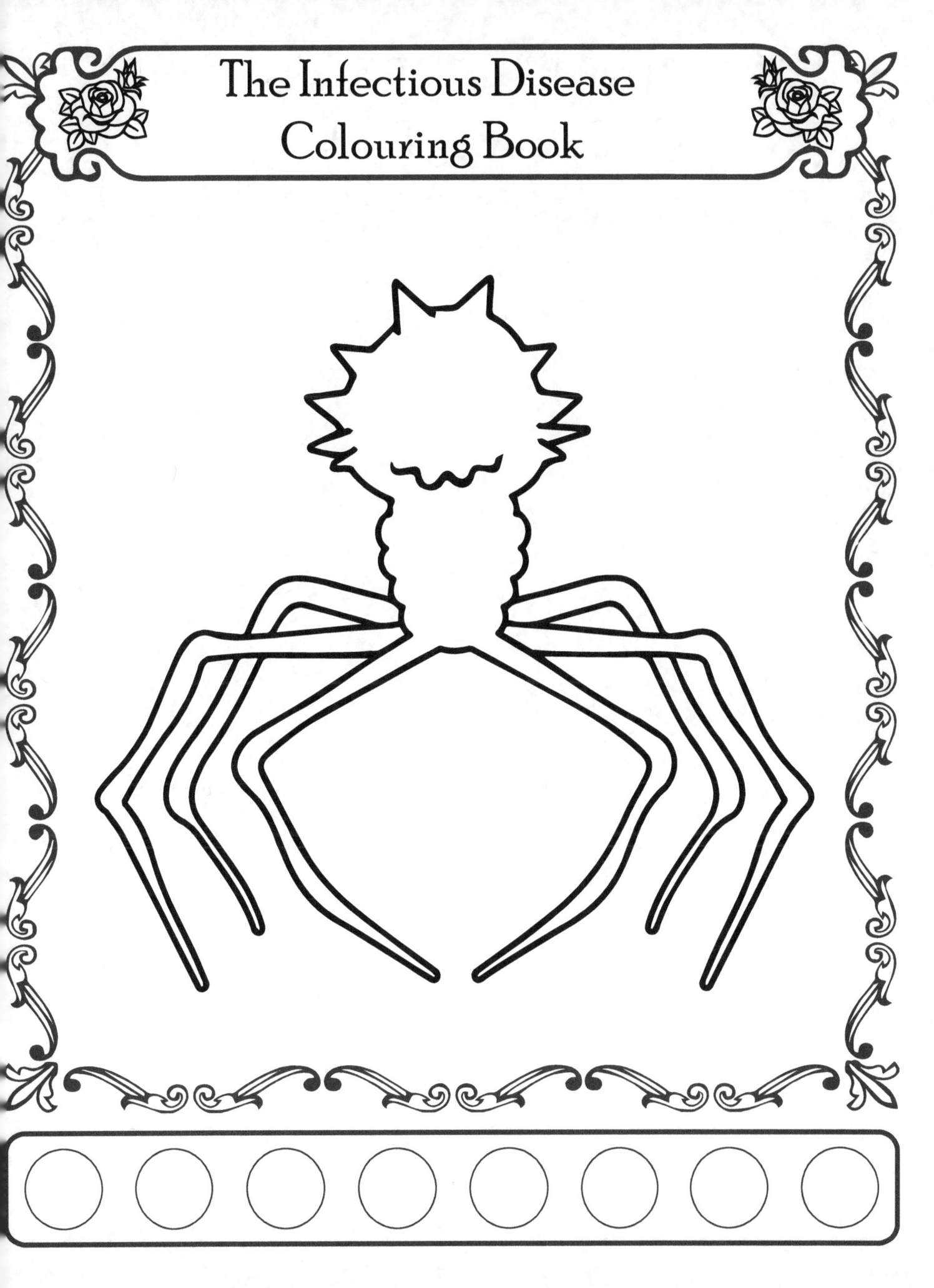

The Infectious Disease Colouring Book

The Infectious Disease Colouring Book

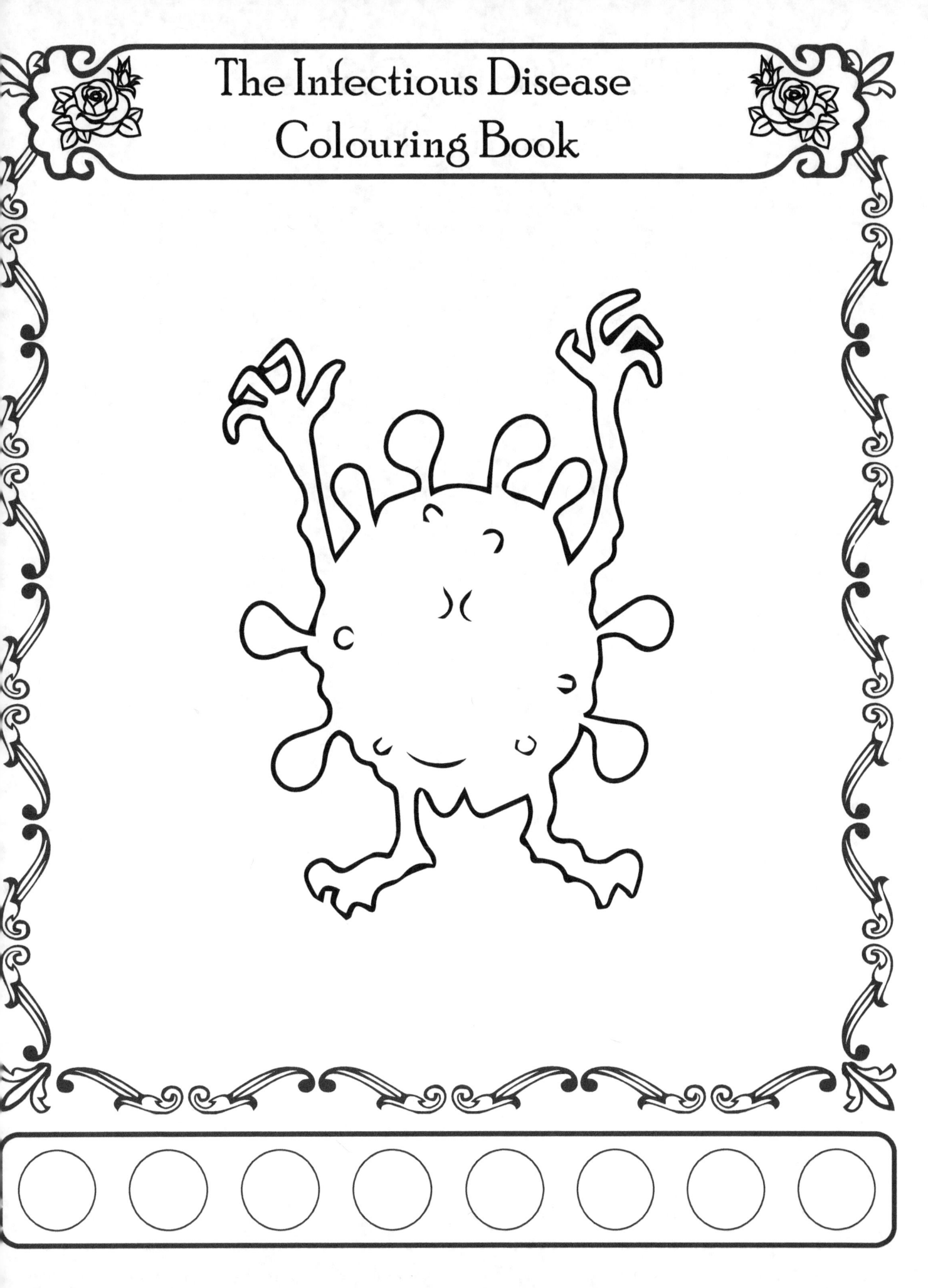

The Infectious Disease Colouring Book

The Infectious Disease Colouring Book

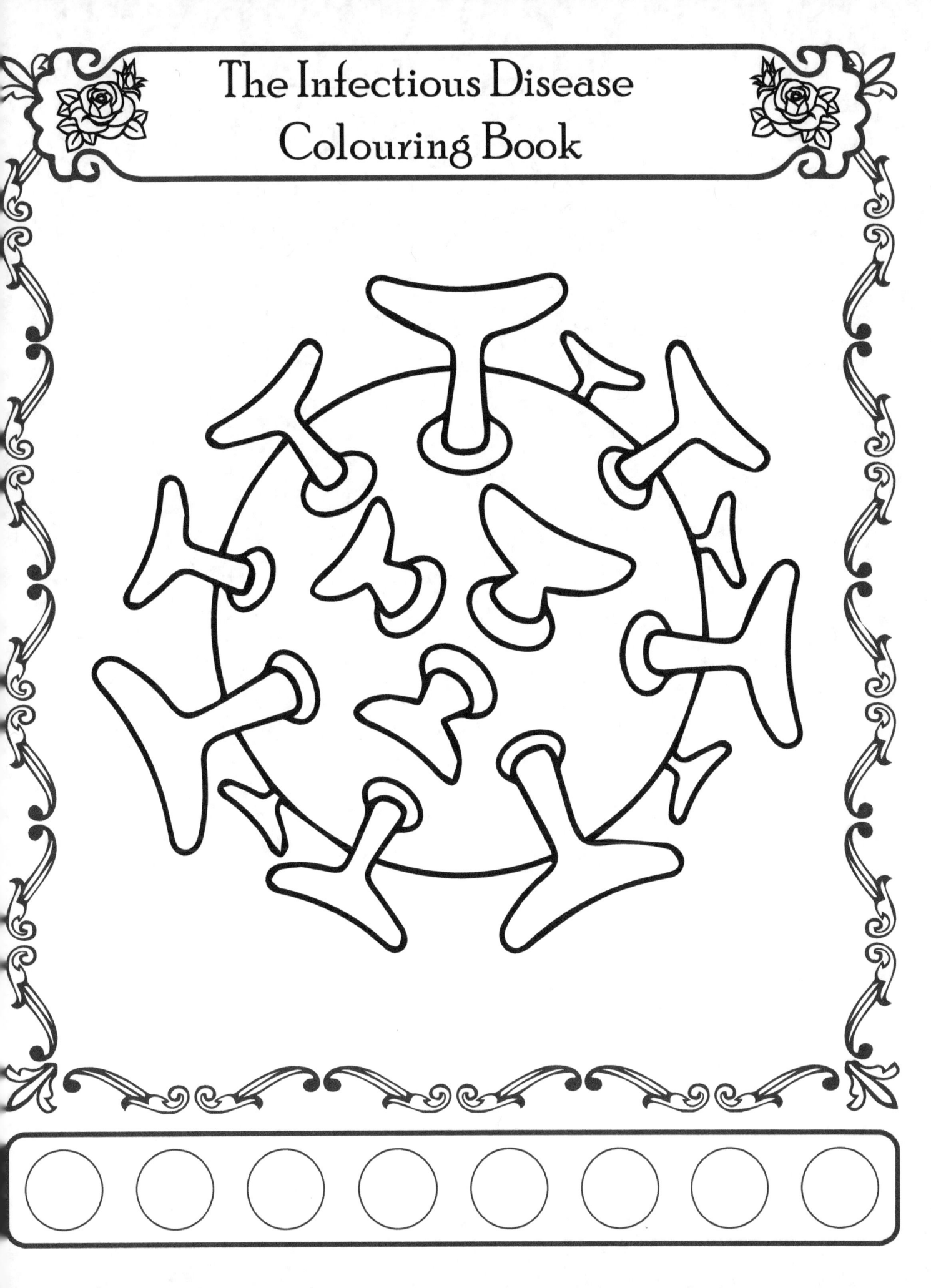

The Infectious Disease Colouring Book

The Infectious Disease Colouring Book

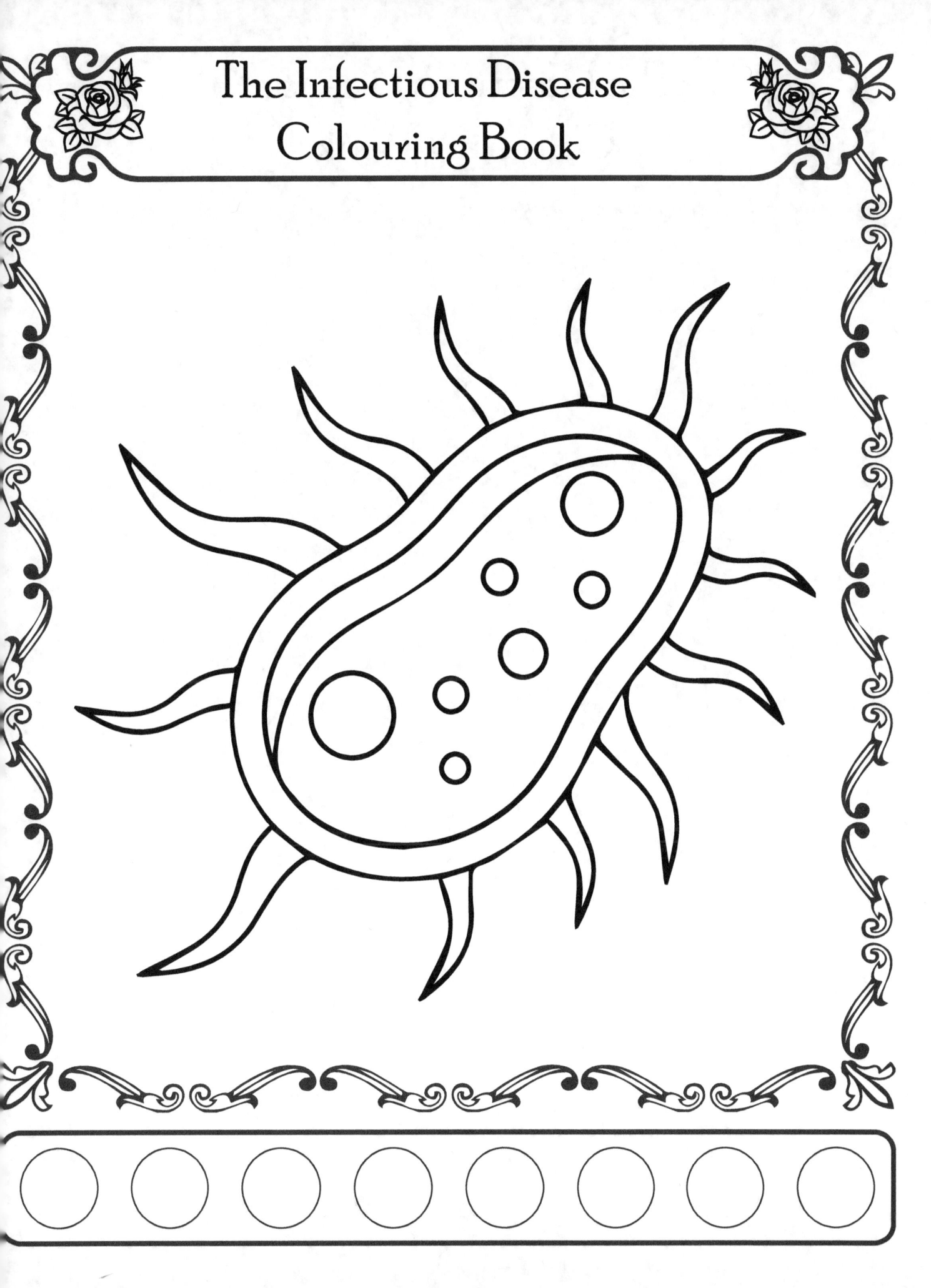

The Infectious Disease
Colouring Book

The Infectious Disease Colouring Book

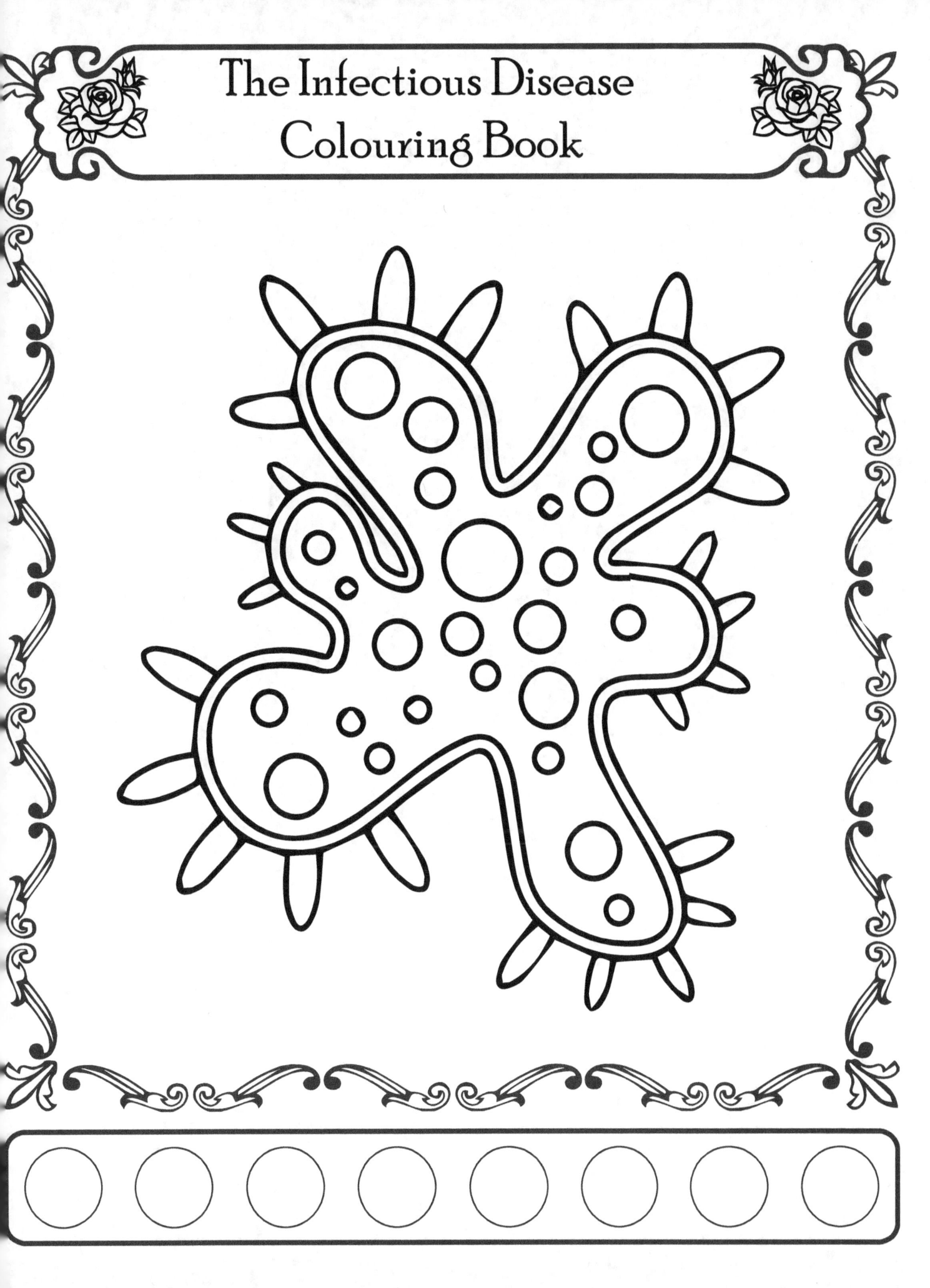

The Infectious Disease Colouring Book

The Infectious Disease Colouring Book

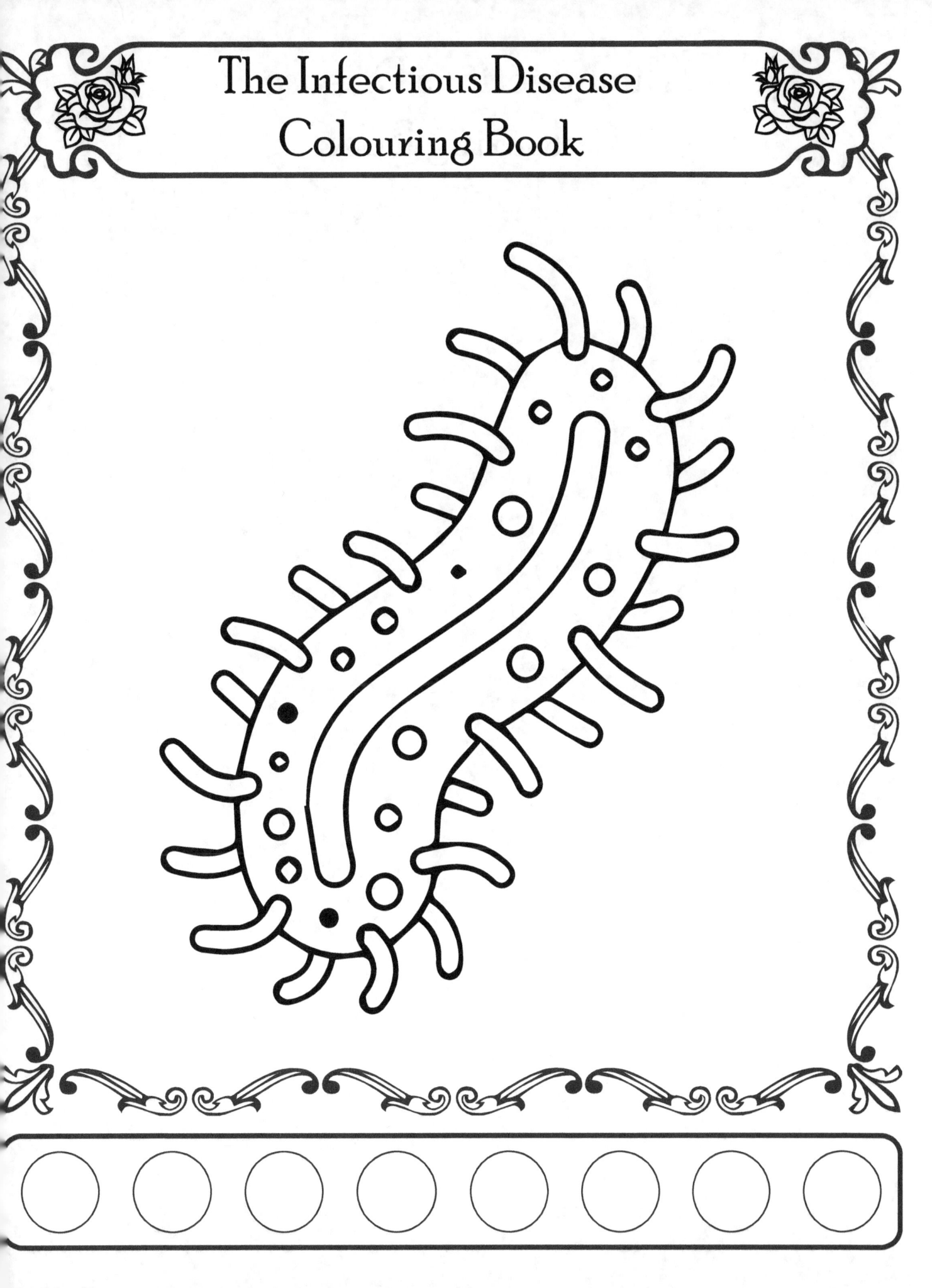

The Infectious Disease
Colouring Book

The Infectious Disease Colouring Book

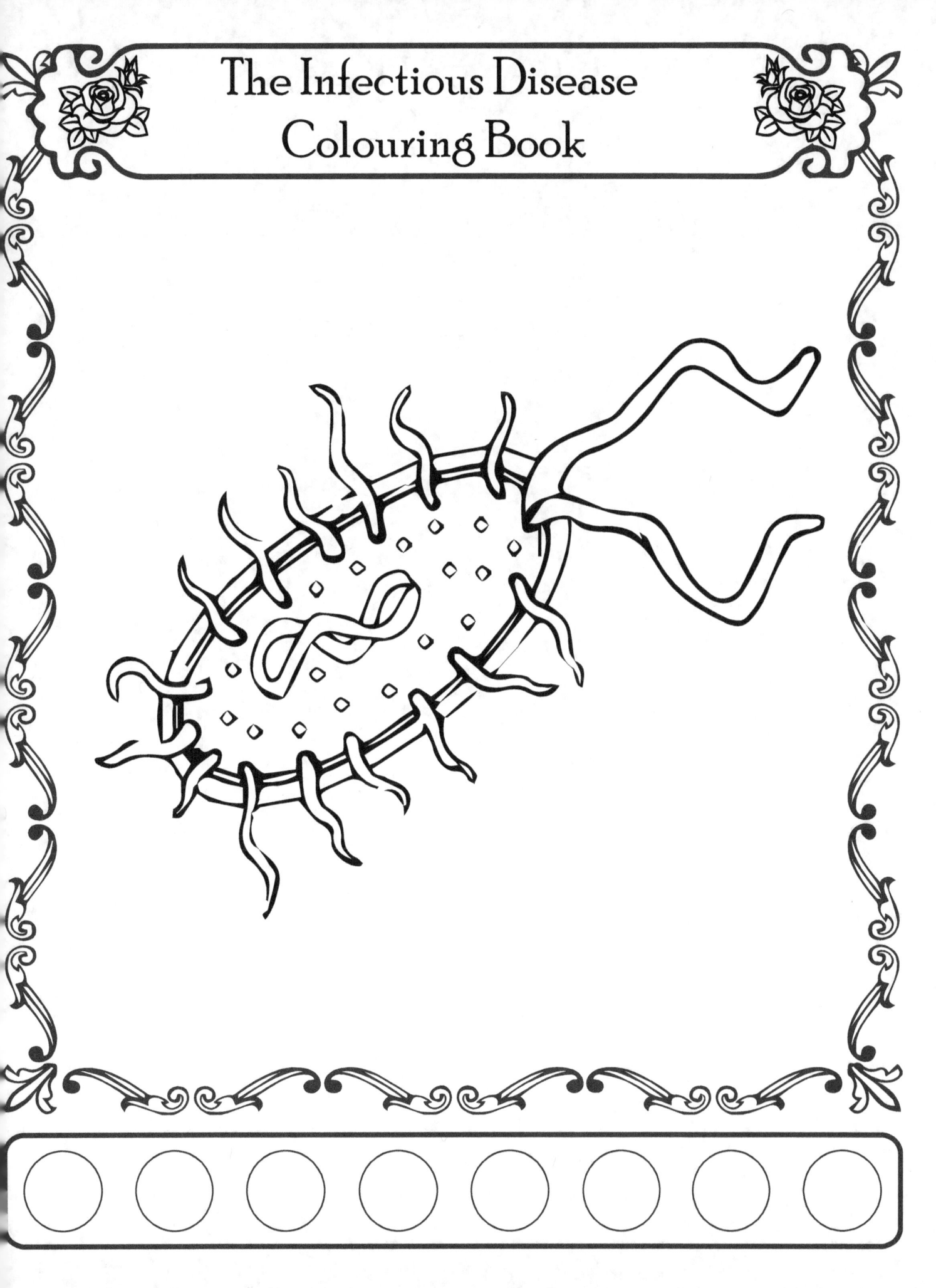

The Infectious Disease
Colouring Book

The Infectious Disease Colouring Book

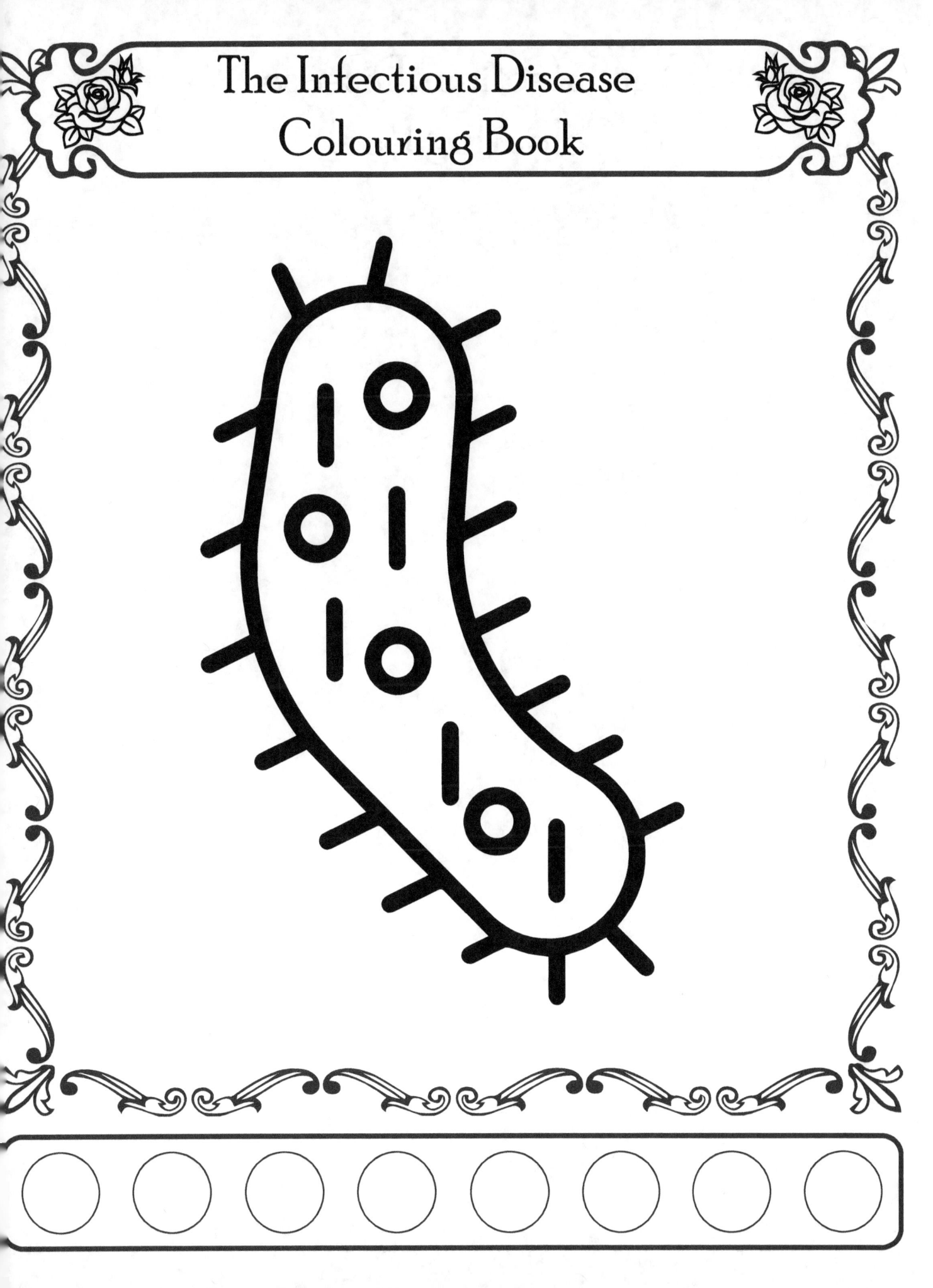

The Infectious Disease Colouring Book

The Infectious Disease Colouring Book

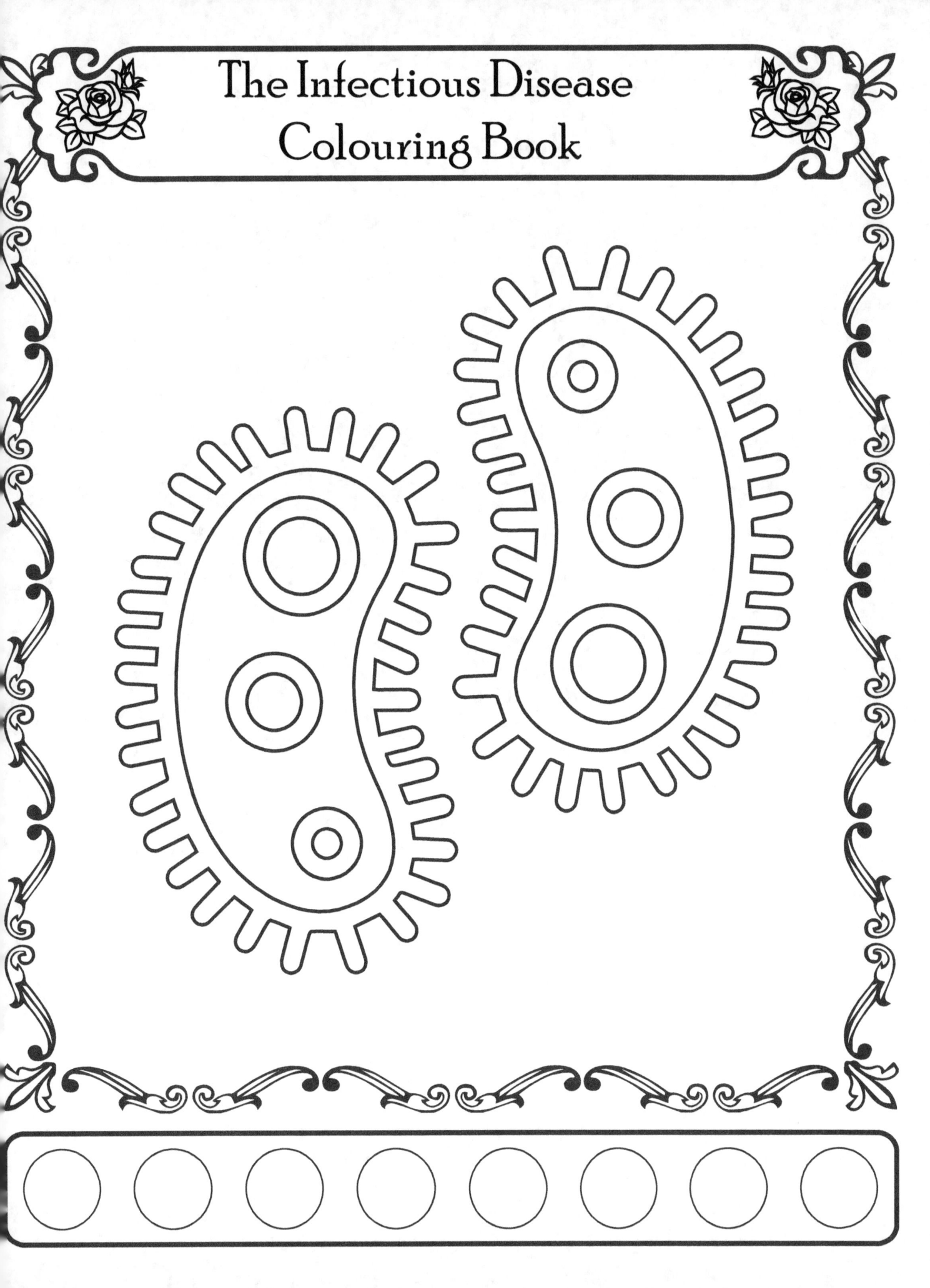

The Infectious Disease Colouring Book

The Infectious Disease Colouring Book

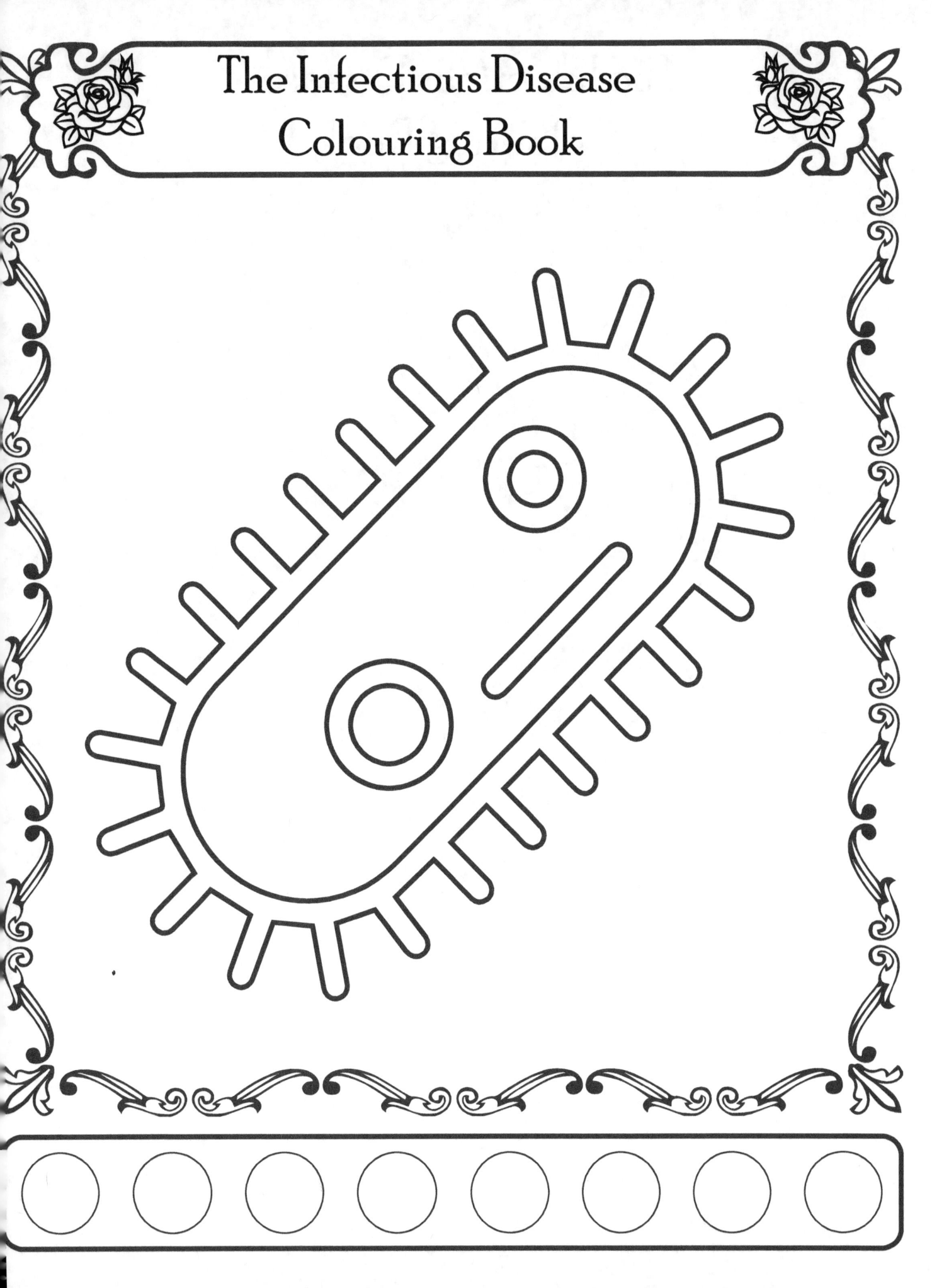

The Infectious Disease Colouring Book

The Infectious Disease Colouring Book

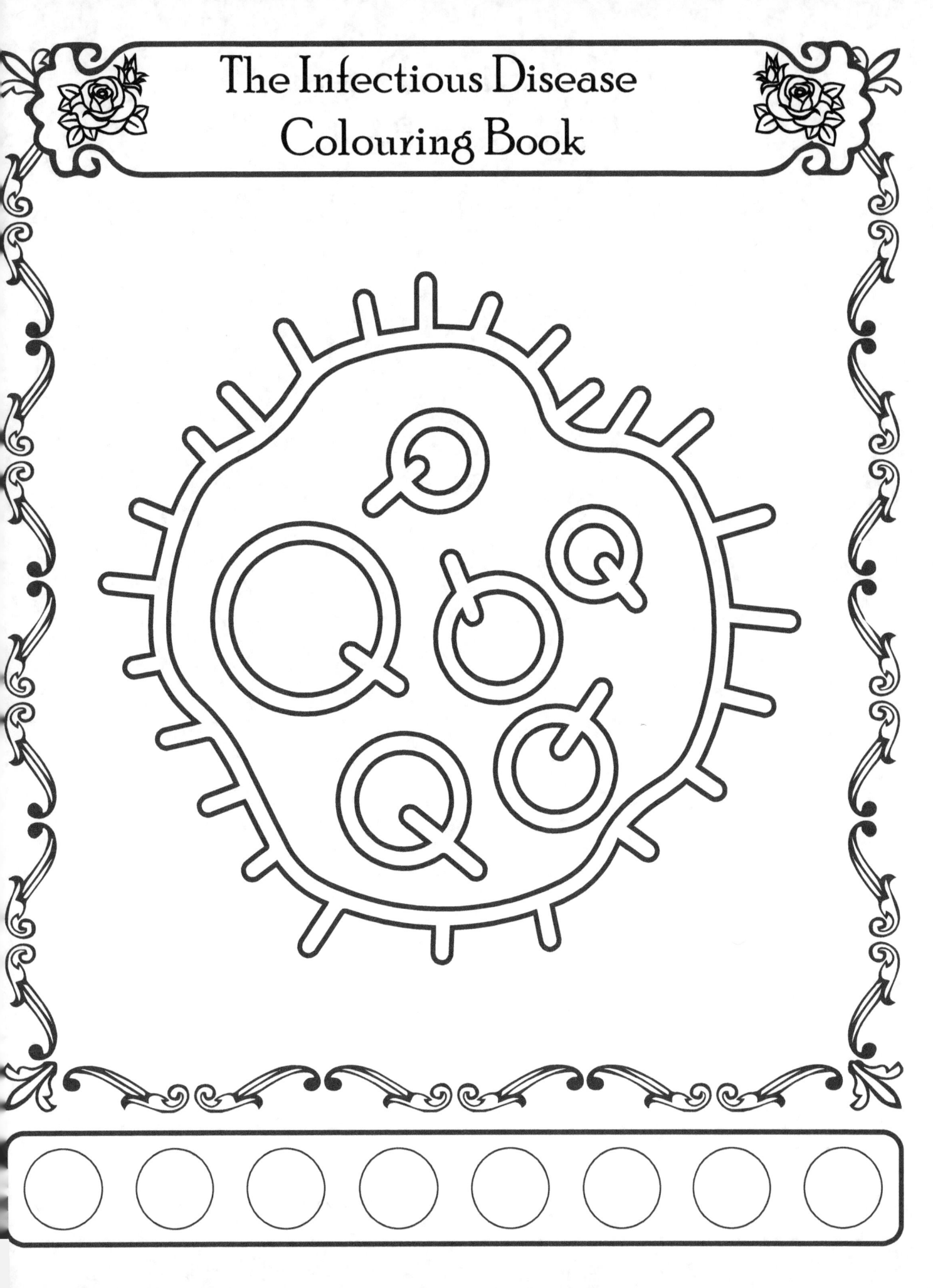

The Infectious Disease Colouring Book

The Infectious Disease Colouring Book

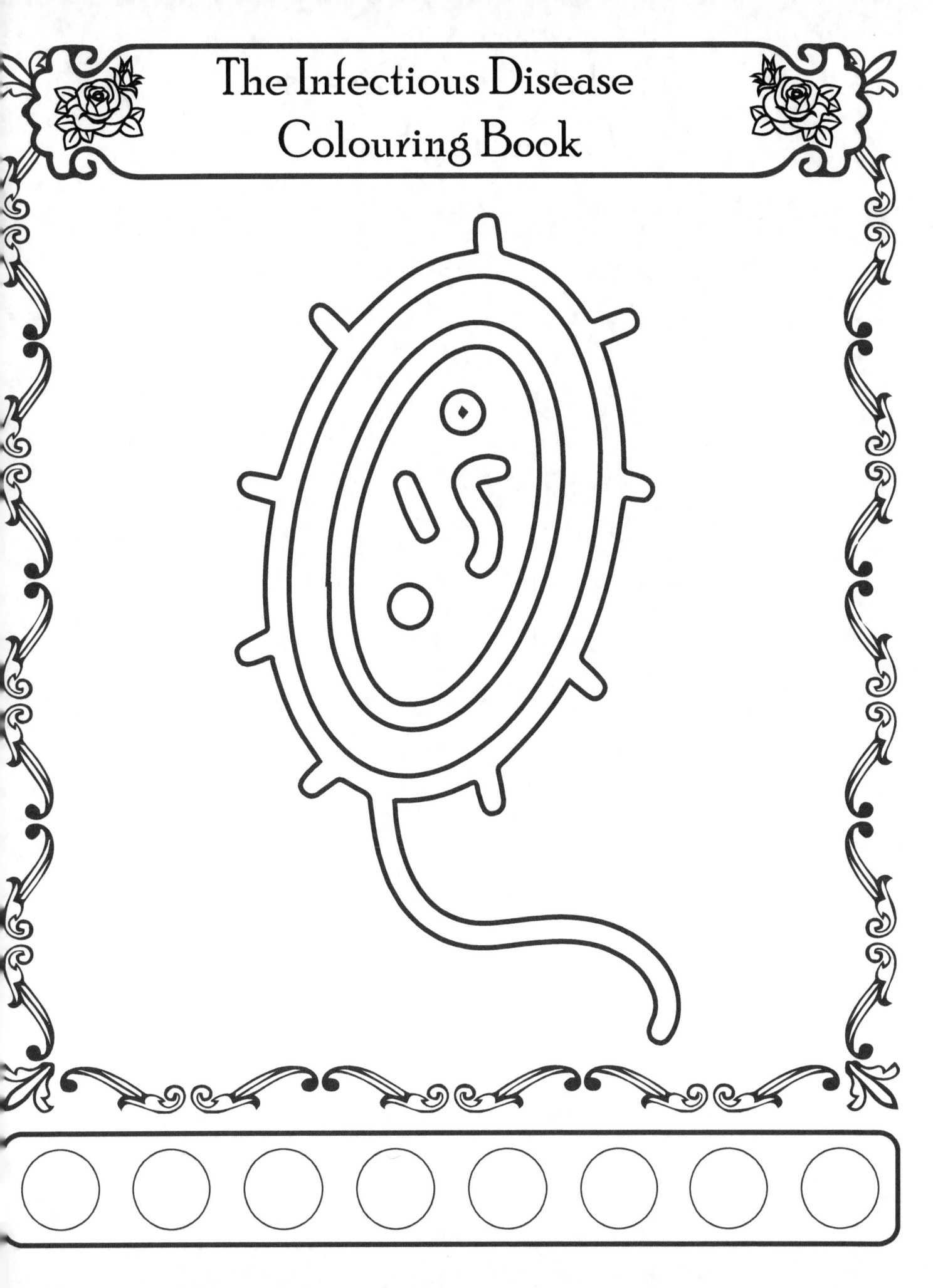

The Infectious Disease
Colouring Book

The Infectious Disease Colouring Book

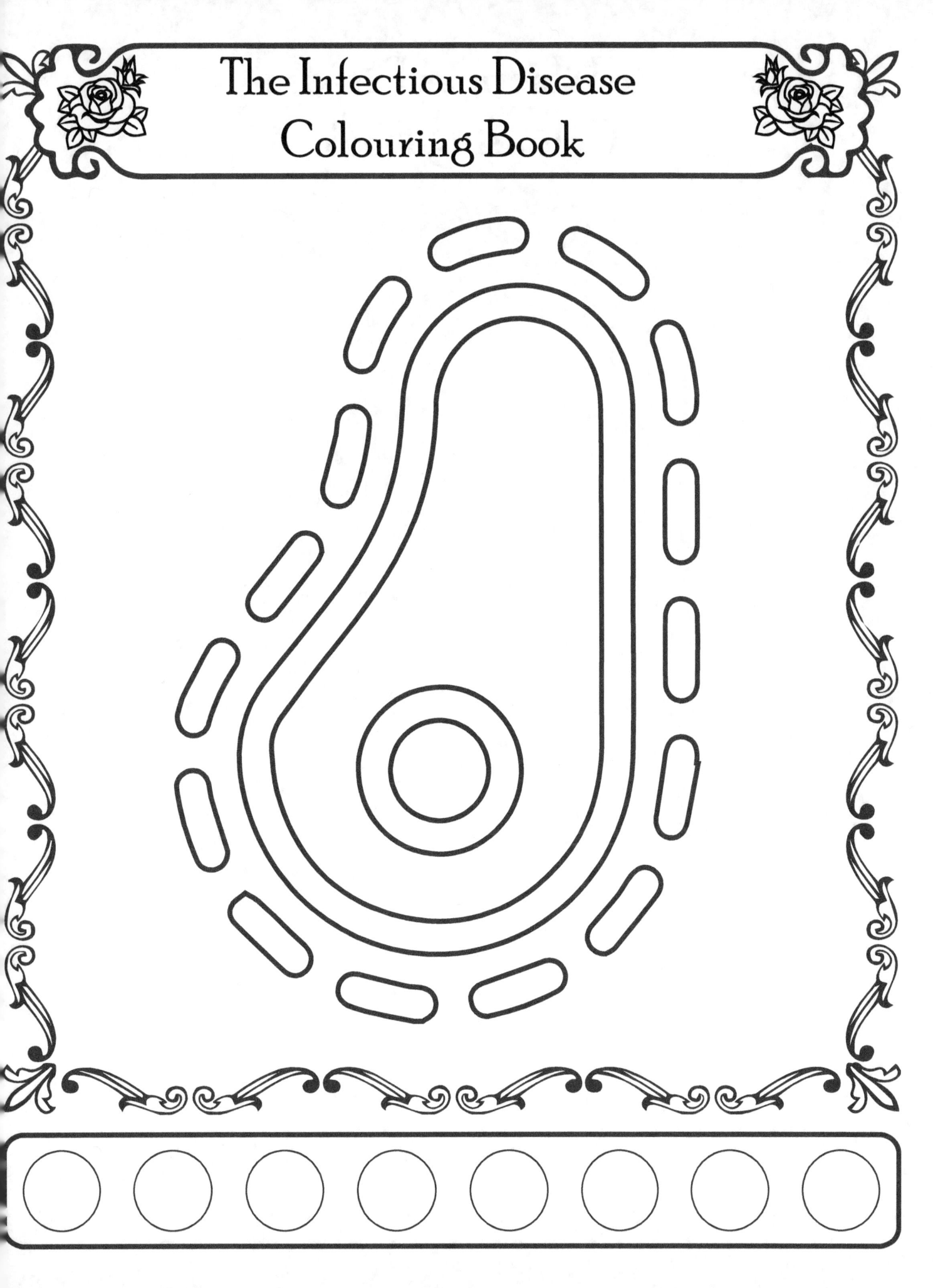

The Infectious Disease Colouring Book

The Infectious Disease Colouring Book

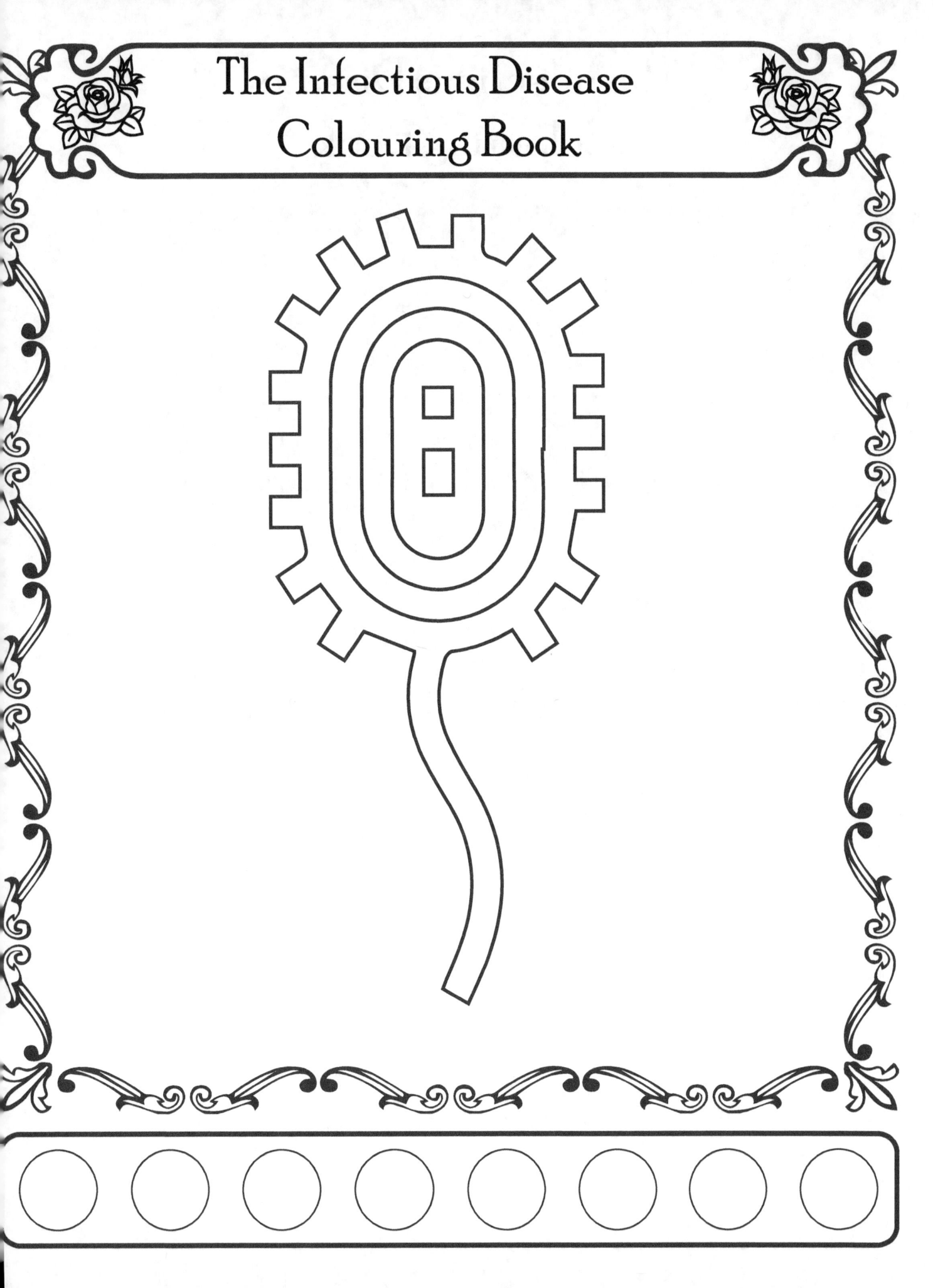

The Infectious Disease
Colouring Book

The Infectious Disease Colouring Book

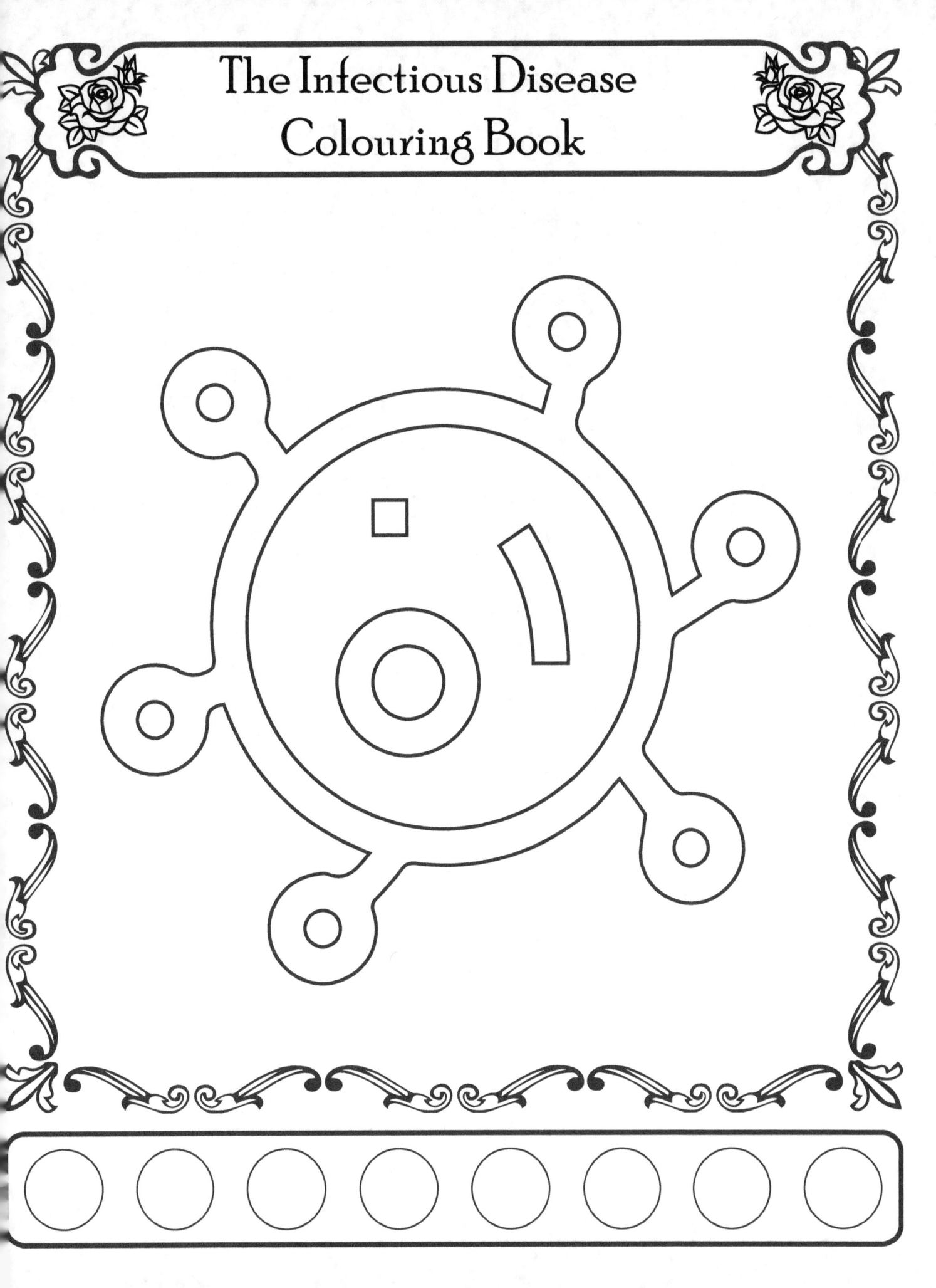

The Infectious Disease
Colouring Book

The Infectious Disease Colouring Book

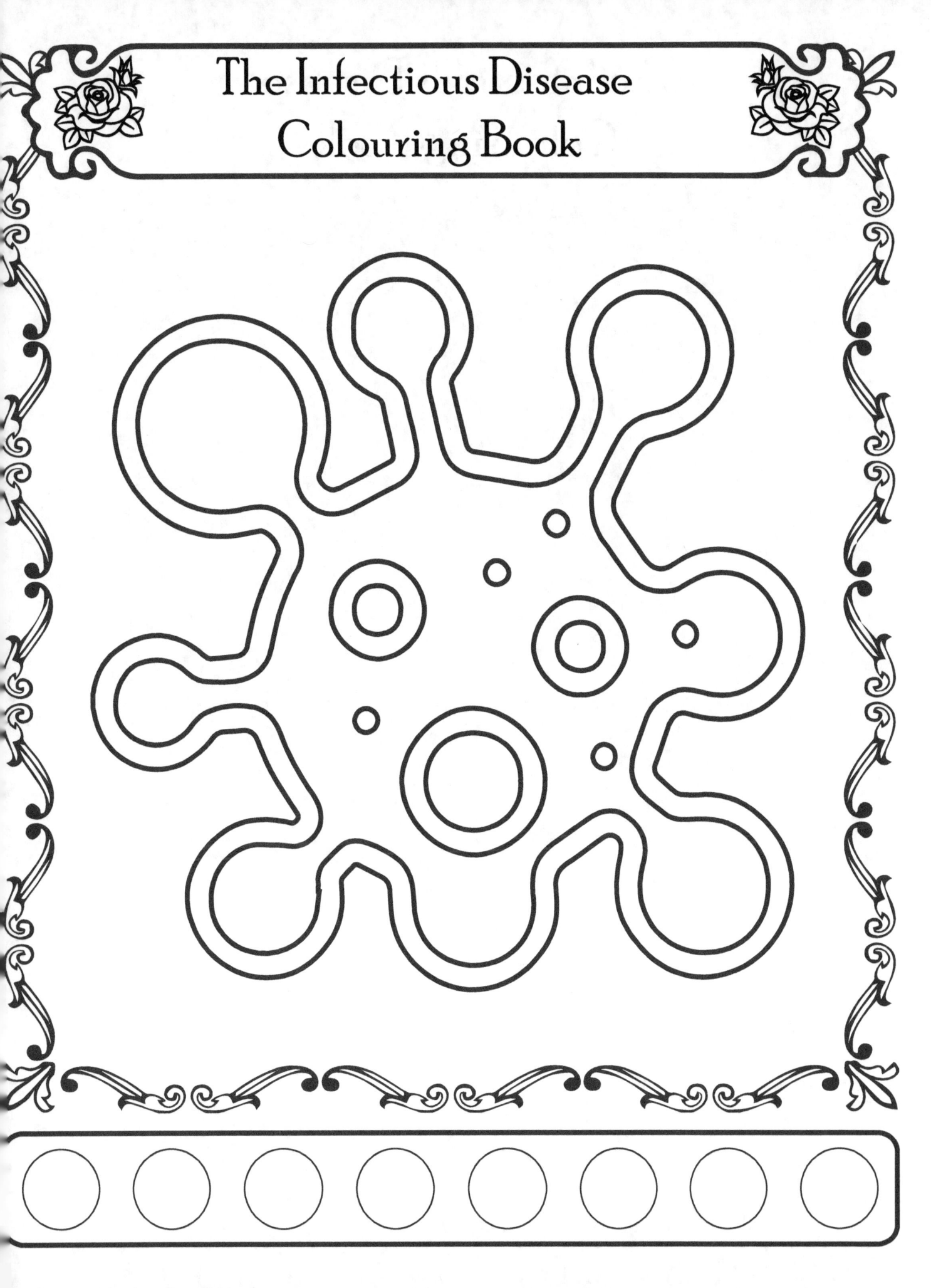

The Infectious Disease
Colouring Book

The Infectious Disease Colouring Book

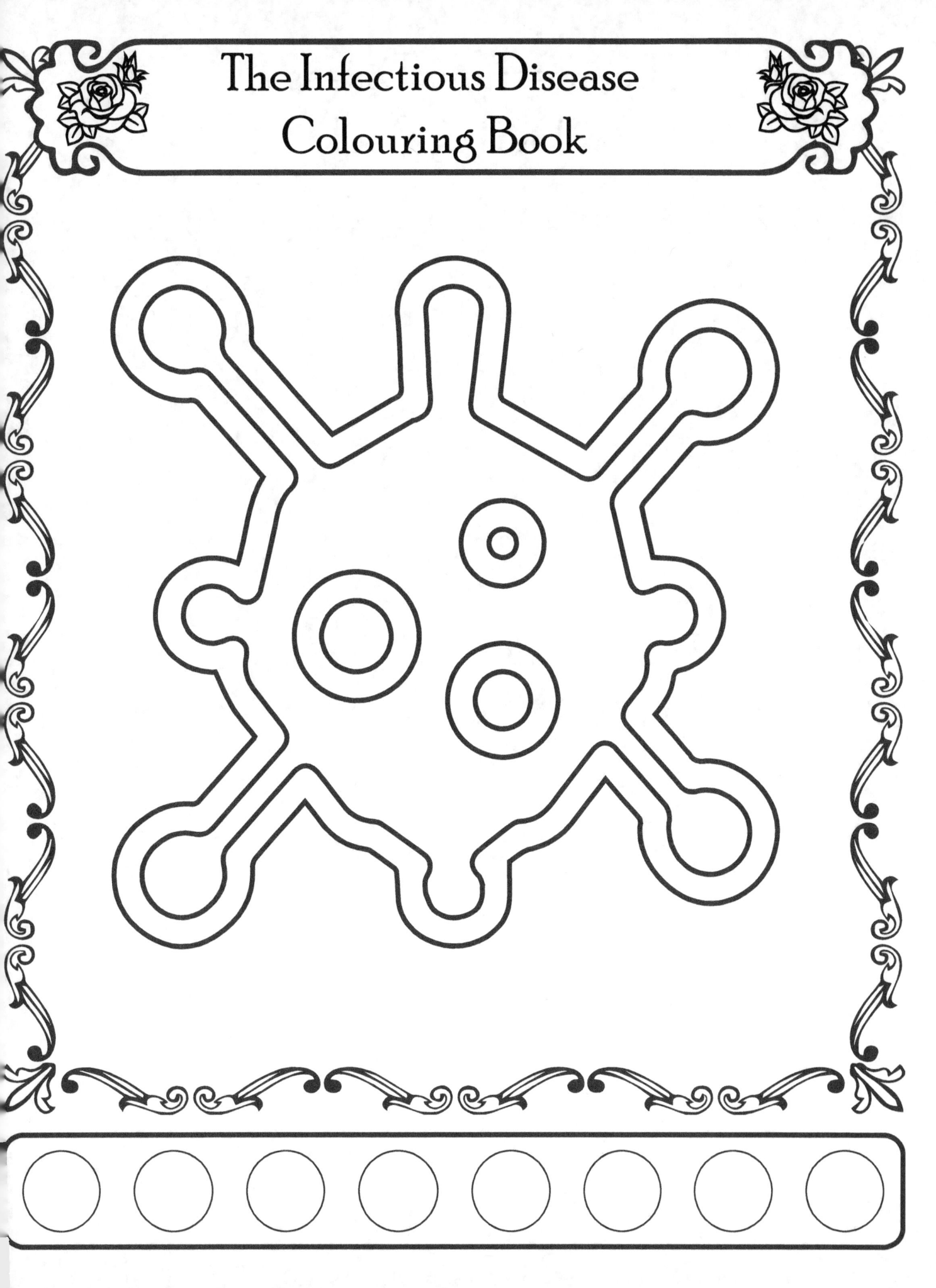

The Infectious Disease Colouring Book

The Infectious Disease Colouring Book

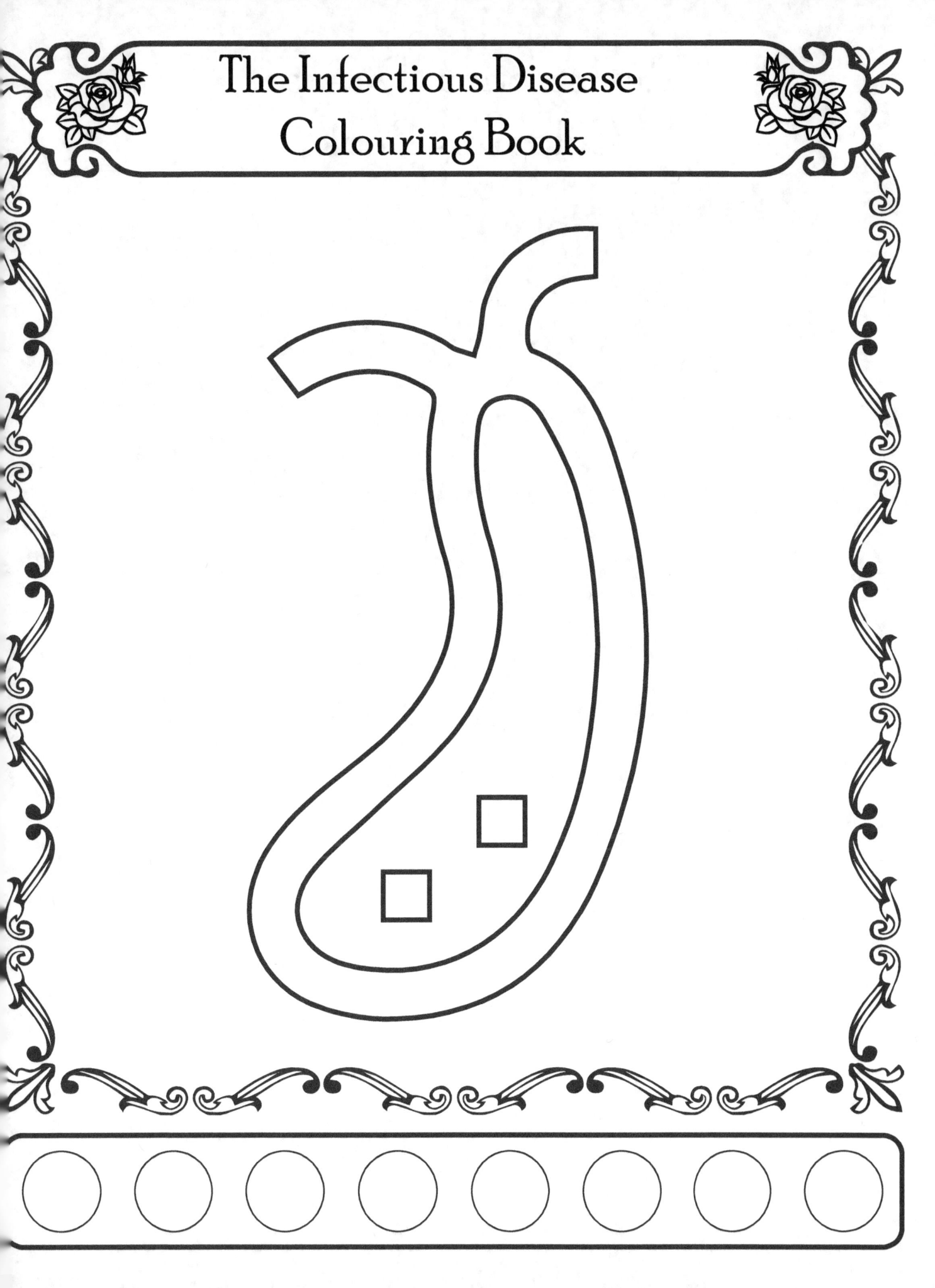

The Infectious Disease
Colouring Book

The Infectious Disease Colouring Book

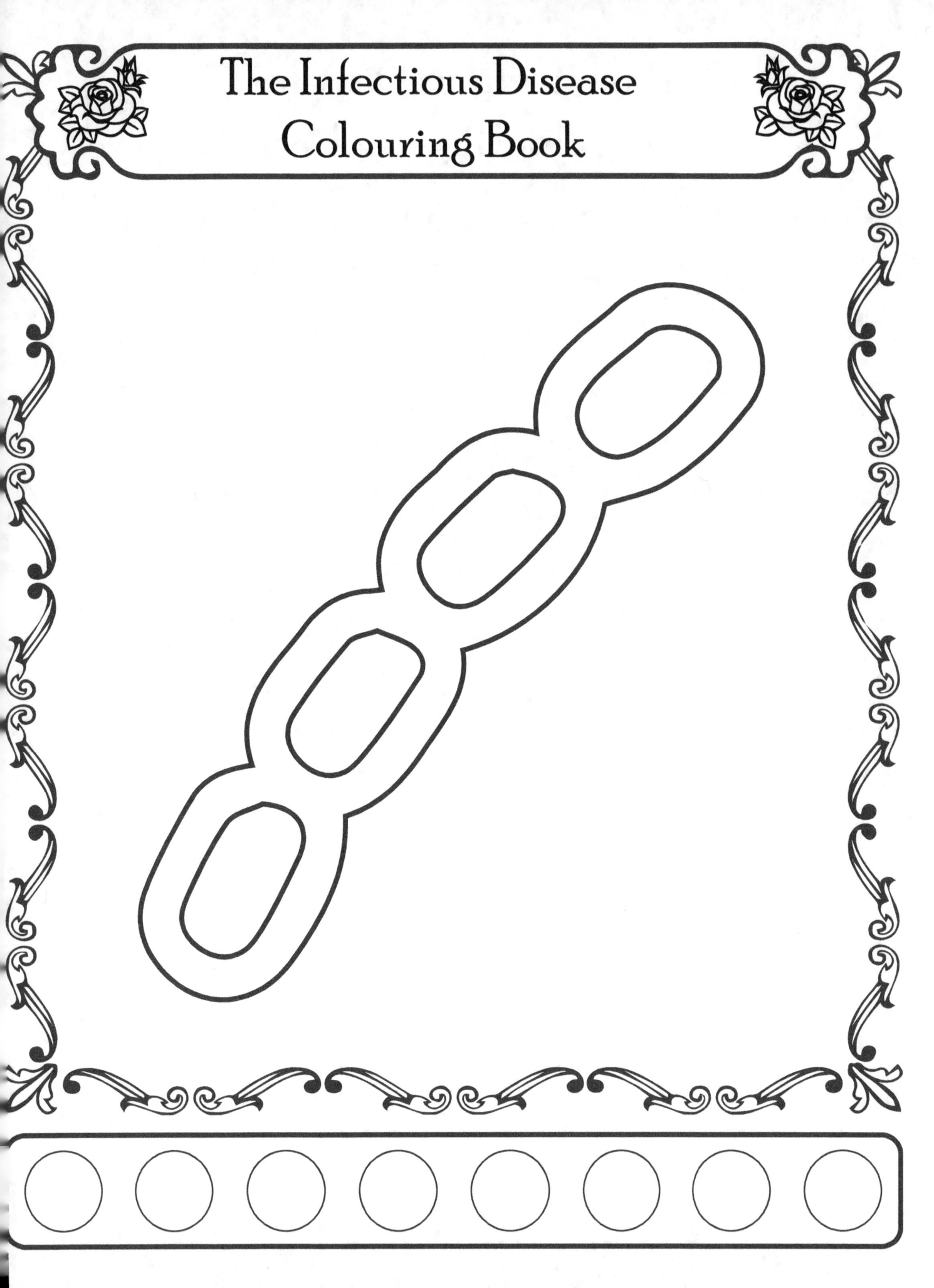

The Infectious Disease
Colouring Book

The Infectious Disease Colouring Book

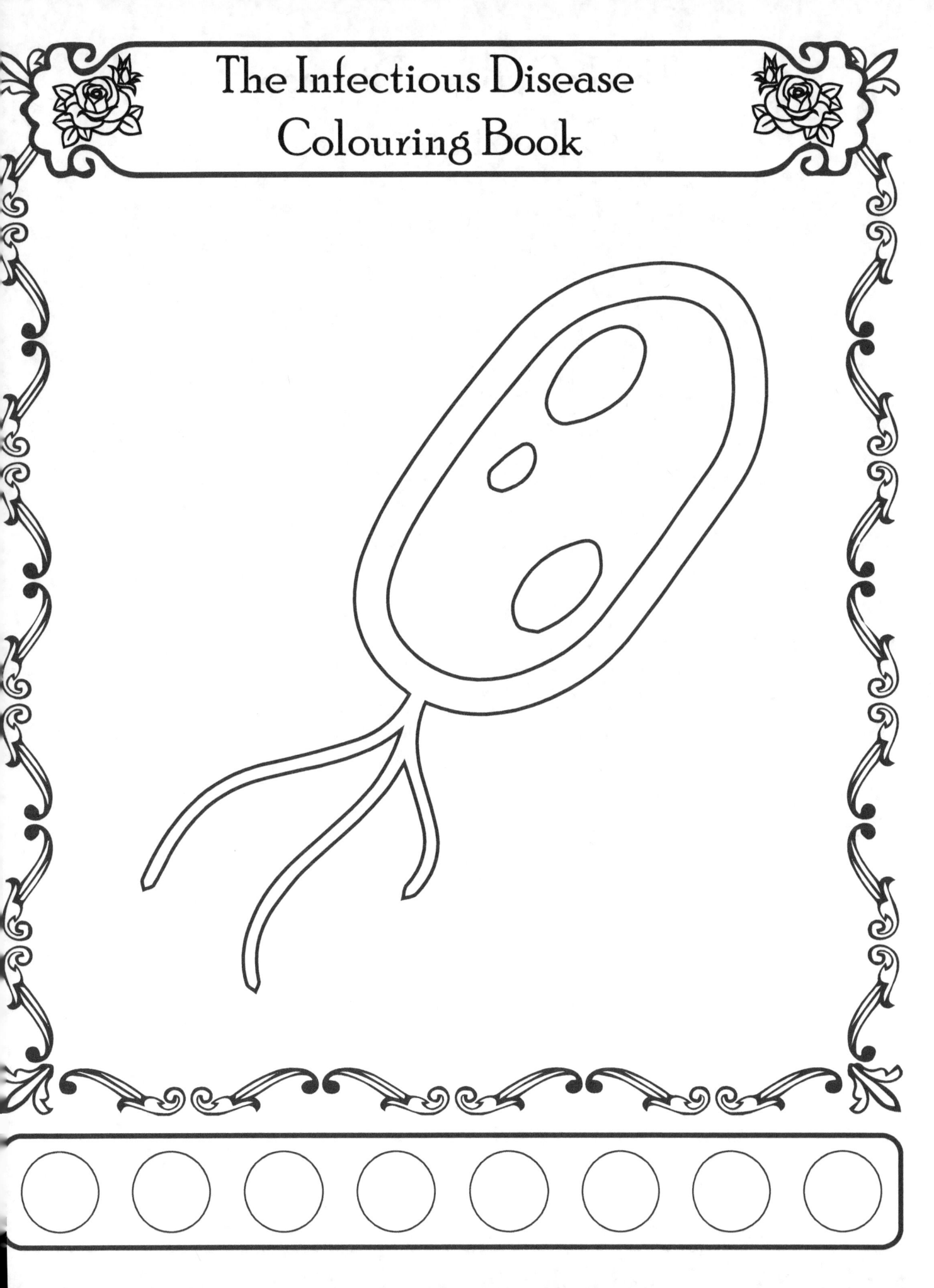

The Infectious Disease Colouring Book

The Infectious Disease Colouring Book

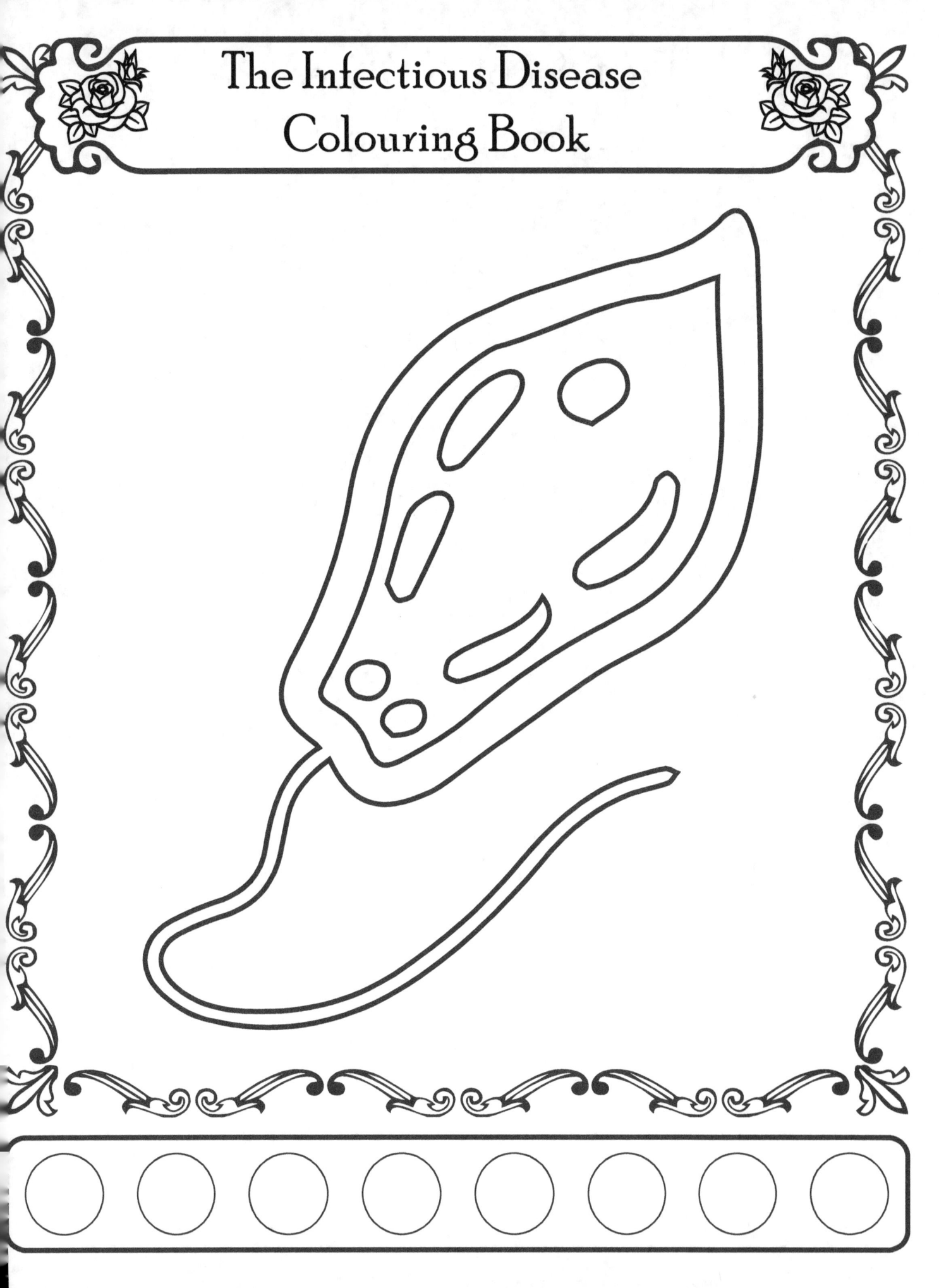

The Infectious Disease
Colouring Book

The Infectious Disease Colouring Book

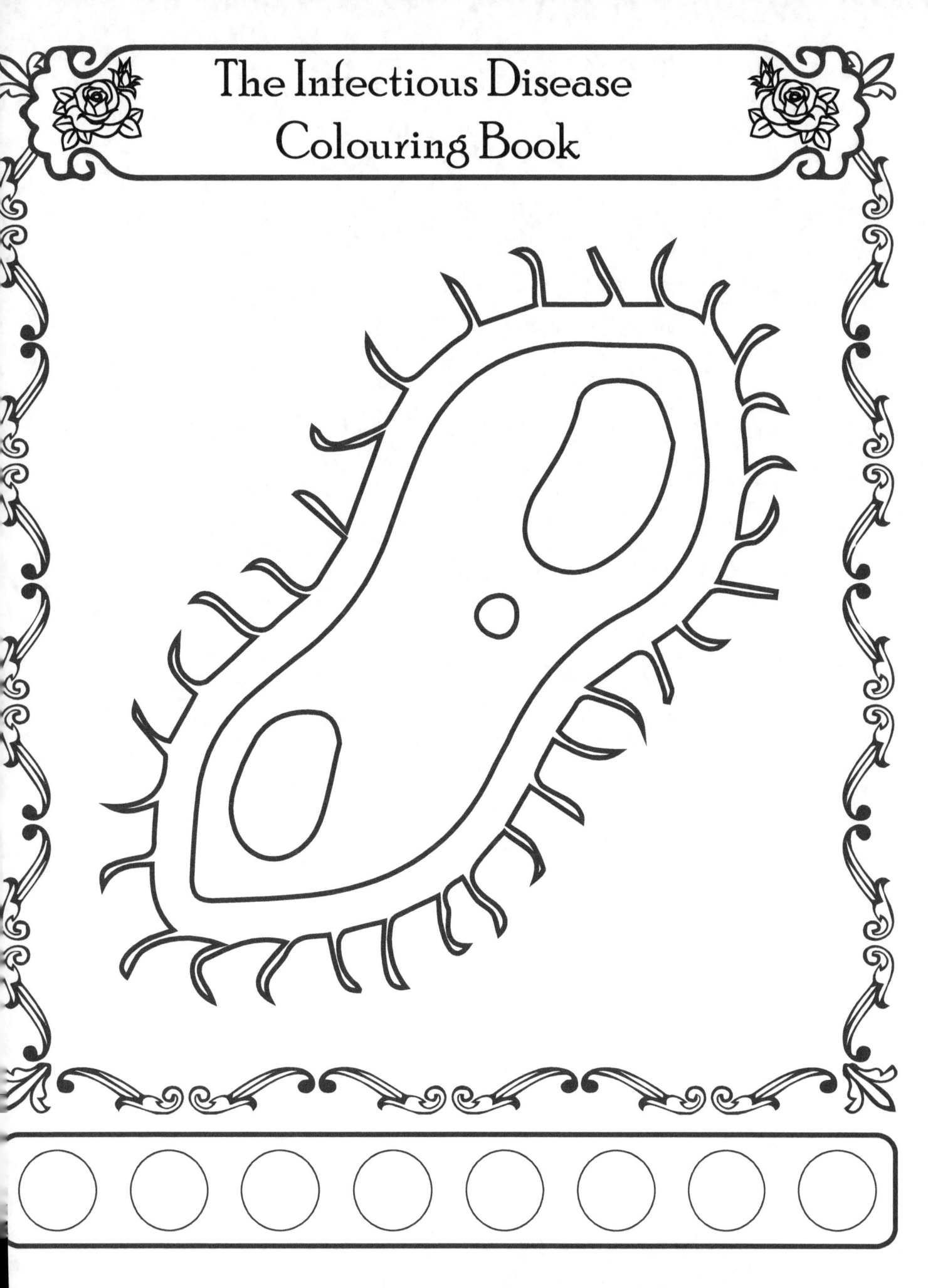

The Infectious Disease
Colouring Book

The Infectious Disease Colouring Book

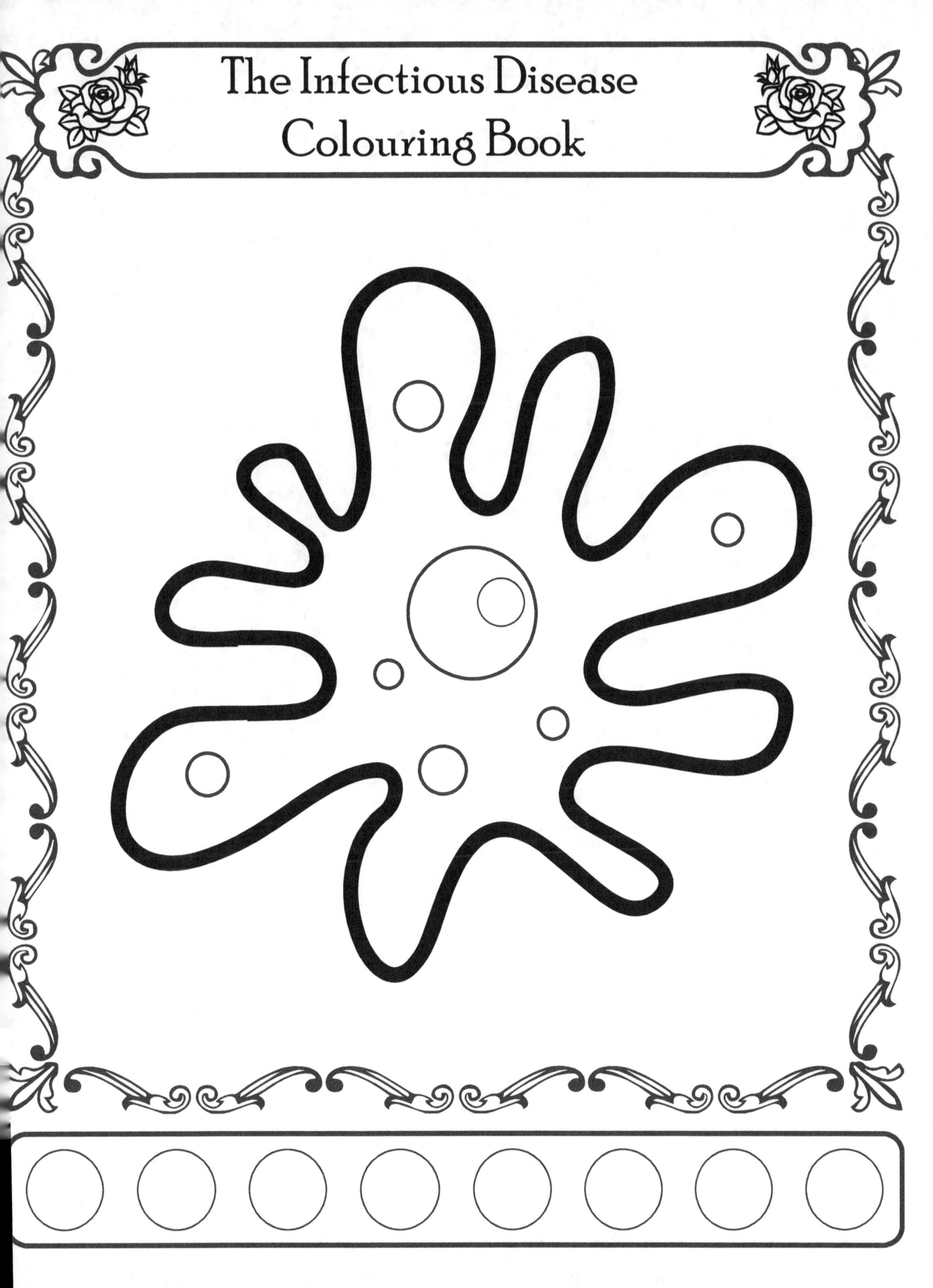

The Infectious Disease
Colouring Book